HARLINGTON

Heydays and Highlights

Edna L. Wilsher

The Book Castle

First published October 2002
by
The Book Castle
12 Church Street
Dunstable
Bedfordshire LU5 4RU

ISBN 1 903747 24 4

Typeset & Designed by Alan R. James

Printed by Antony Rowe Ltd., Chippenham, Wiltshire

Cover picture reproduced courtesy of Harlington Parochial Church Council
and Woodmansterne Publications Ltd.

CONTENTS

Dedication

Dedicated to all the villagers of Harlington, past, present and future. Also to my husband Andy, to whom I give my special thanks for his long-suffering and patience while this book was being written.

Introduction.

Harlington, Bedfordshire is the village of my birth where I started out on my journey through life to the new millennium and beyond. A journey which reached out to other places, but always brought me back to the little village that was my home. Featured in this story are the days of childhood, bringing me into contact with the famous legacy of John Bunyan, author of "The Pilgrim's Progress." Moving on from childhood, the next stage was the wartime years in Harlington and my service days which took me away from the village, followed eventually by my journalistic years on a local newspaper, leading to marriage and eventually to the millennium itself with its celebratory events.

Time has brought many changes to villages that were once small and Harlington is no exception. Since I started out on my journey hundreds of houses have appeared where the green fields were once seen and enjoyed by children at play. Incomers of the later years now live alongside the Old Harlingtonians. They have brought with them a faster way of life, new ideas and activities, not a bad thing in many ways. But the spirit of Old Harlington lingers still, for although the Bunyan tree from which John Bunyan is said to have preached is in its skeletal state, there are still wild flowers to be found if you know where to look for them!

Harlington is said to be Anglo-Saxon in origin. It stands high on a hill looking out towards the part of the Chilterns once known as Markham Hills but now called Sundon Hills Country Park with its neighbouring Sharpenhoe Clappers. In the Domesday Book of 1086 in the Hundred of Manshead, it is recorded as "Herlingdone," meaning "Hill of Herela's People." We all know that many years ago invaders crossed the seas to our shores, but who Herela was is best left to the history books.

I wish to thank the following for their help and the use of information given in this book:

Mr. R. Hedley; Mr. E. Huckle; Joan Giles; the late John Giles; Ken Giles; Richard and Pat Dudley; Jack and Margaret Hewitt; Brian and Ada Letting; Rita and Alan Hart; Dorothy Preston; Jessie Delve; Ruby Hillyard; Joan Groom; Brenda Platt; Kitty Chambers; Kate Geraghty (nee Whiskin); Ida Kendall; Mrs. Eleanor Lee; Ann Dunn.

Other sources of information:
Bedfordshire and Luton Archives and Record Services;
The Dunstable Methodist Circuit 1843-1993. c1993; Survey of Bedfordshire Brickmaking (Alan Cox. Nov. 1979); Harlington in Camera. Russell Preston; Harlington in Camera (2) Russell Preston and Stephen Castle; Harlington Parish Church Archives; The Parish of St. Mary the Virgin Church Guide. Harlington 1989. Russell Preston; Harlington Heritage Trust (A Brief History of Harlington Newsletter 75. John Thurston); Home Counties Newspapers Ltd. (Luton at War); Kelly's Directories; Mrs. Mary Rutherford, Parish Clerk Harlington Parish Council; Angela Hillyard, personal interview c. 2000 "Harlington Arms."; Kettering Tourist Information Centre; P3 Footpath Leaflets. Local history Cards. Russell Preston.

Grateful thanks to the following who supplied or permitted the use of photographs:
Stephen Castle; Christine Sheed; Rita Hart; Russell Preston; Cliff Stone; Andrew Wilsher; Ann Dunn; L. Justice; Brenda Platt; Luton News.

Special thanks also to Russell Preston for computer expertise and to Angela Hillyard for her encouragement throughout the writing of this book.

The Bunyan Tree.

The Bunyan Tree was broad and strong
When I was young.
Its branches reached out green and wide
Like arms outflung,
Protecting hills and fields from where
It firmly stood.
Of times long past, a symbol there
Of all that's good.

How often did I climb the 'steps'
Smoothed out in wood
To where that man, so great a preacher
Once had stood!
How often did our little group of
Children Play,
Pretend to give a sermon on a
Summer day!

And though the years have passed
Yet still we see
What now remains, a skeleton
Of Bunyan's Tree;
But in another form its beauty
Still is there -
One mighty limb into an altar made
So sculptured rare.

St. Mary's you are blessed indeed
To have this part
To keep within your hallowed walls
This Sacred Art.

Edna L. Wilsher.

Note - The 'steps' were a faint indentation as though someone had continually climbed to an inner part of the tree which looked suspiciously like a natural pulpit of wood.

The new village sign of Harlington, erected for the millennium year 2000.
The picture shows John Bunyan beneath an oak tree, with open book
("The Pilgrim's Progress.") The second half portrays children reading,
in the background a sheaf of corn, a green train and cottages of yesteryear.

Photo: R. Preston.

Chapter One

Old Familiar Places

The little red leaflet on display at the village post office was the beginning of it all - the surge of memory that swept over me at the mention of my own village of Harlington, Bedfordshire, where my ancestry on both sides of my parentage lay.

My grandfather, John Frederick Lane, had been a Harlingtonian; also my father, John Albert Lane, who was baptised in the Church of St. Mary the Virgin and from a lad onwards sang in the choir until a late age. He was a bellringer there and he attended the little village school. My maternal grandmother Lucy Brinklow, was the oldest child of my great grandfather, Truman Brinklow of Harlington. He and his wife

1

had a large family. Lucy left the village on her marriage to live in Sheffield, but my mother came back to her roots to marry my father in Harlington Church - because she had more relatives in Harlington than in Sheffield - and remained there.

Parental Grandparents Lane

Thus it was that I was born in Harlington, the village renowned for its John Bunyan connection. I was baptised in the Church of St. Mary the Virgin as my father had been and attended the same little village school.

Nostalgia swept over me as my eyes scanned the words on the little red leaflet. It told me that the Fortnum and Mason 1995 Window displays based on the theme of John Bunyan's book "The Pilgrim's Progress" were to be seen in the Church of St. Mary the Virgin, Harlington, Bedfordshire, from February 1996 to the first week in November 1996 (actually, the public were so drawn to this wonderful gift, given to the Church after Fortnum and Mason no longer required it, that it was kept on much longer.) I decided it was not to be missed. My own connections with John Bunyan's life would have attracted me if nothing else had.

Maternal Grandparents Lummna

As a child I would run across the fields to a certain tree called John Bunyan's Oak because tradition had it that he climbed to what appeared to be a natural pulpit of wood inside the tree and spoke to the gathering crowd. It was a great novelty for me to run up the steps (a faint indentation in the tree leading to the pulpit) and pretend to be the renowned evangelist, my listeners being my own young friends. I was not the only child to do that. Others in the village loved to do the same thing. It was exciting. It was exhilarating.

I had been living in Scotland for a short number of years and now, coming back to Bedfordshire I was going to catch up on a few things so long stored in my memory.

So it was that I found myself tootling along the road in a car to Harlington from its neighbouring village of Silsoe where I was living. The autumn sun shone through the window and the leaves were just turning to the season's rich golden-russet shades. It was indeed a heavenly, relaxed afternoon, set fair for the memorable visit that lay ahead of me.

Parents - Lane

There were very few cars on the road, so the village of Barton-le-Clay was passed through at a gentle speed, and I glanced at that part of the range of Chiltern hills which, it is said by some, are the "Delectable Mountains" John Bunyan wrote about in "The Pilgrim's Progress." Now they are called "Barton Hills" and further along, "Sundon Hills," but when I was young they were known as "The Sharpenhoe Clappers" and "Markham Hills," the latter where we used to picnic. At the top of Sundon hill Road on the way down to Harlington, there is now a car park

4

so that people can walk the stretch towards the hills. This is now called "Sundon Hills Country Park." Again, when I was young we walked from Harlington, Sundon Road, round what is known as "The Bottoms," presumably because it was at the bottom of Harlington, then turning right through a gateway, along a cart track to the steep climb up to the hills.

A feeling that heightened within me as the car bowled along the Barton Road at the top of Harlington village made me wind down the window. It was hot in the car with the sun streaming in. The autumn air was glorious. It was then that memories of years past came flooding back so vividly as I gazed at the scene of my earlier days. The car sped on, round the corner to Harlington Church which stood opposite the modern vicarage, so different from the old vicarage I remembered.

The Revd Stephen J. Williams escorted me into the Church where the most impressive display met my gaze, glorious and golden, depicting John Bunyan's story of "The Pilgrim's Progress." He then showed me the Communion table and told me the story of how it came to be made from part of the oak tree from which John Bunyan preached in 1660, the tree of my childhood. It is a remarkable story of how, in the devastating storm of 1987 that ravaged the countryside, a great limb had been torn asunder from the tree. But it had been put to a wonderful use. The story seeped into my heart and mind so that when I reached home I found myself sitting at my typewriter and writing the Bunyan Tree poem. It was indeed a very deep and spiritual experience.

I left the Church of St. Mary the Virgin standing sentinel and majestic in the autumnal sunshine. Along the road, there was the old Bunyan Tree in its field, looking sad but still very proud, bare "arms" outstretched to the hills, just a skeleton of what it used to be those long years ago. Services have taken place at the Bunyan Oak tree through the years and many

5

people have visited it from different countries. In 1988 over five hundred people turned up to witness a new oak sapling being planted beside the dear old Bunyan's Oak by the naturalist Dr. David Bellamy. With a lump in my throat, I looked at the skeleton of the old tree.

The Oak Tree

That visit back to Harlington left its mark on me. I was taken back in time to the years when I looked out of my bedroom window and gazed across to the hills. To me they spelled laughter and fun with my fellow playmates and our families - the picnics we had up there in the summer, the journey along the dusty road to that magical spot where we lit our camp fire for a day, the smell of delicious fat sausages sizzling in the pan on the camp fire and a thousand other things. And then I found myself thinking back even further, transported to a little cottage with a vastly different outlook on the opposite side of Harlington, the place where I was born and spent the very earliest days of my life ...

Chapter Two

Earliest years

Bute Cottages were built in 1906 on what was then a trackway before being made into Westoning Road, one of the oldest roads in Harlington. It is a road that I remember and it was in the second of the Bute Cottages that I was born.

Bute Cottages

I also vaguely remember in my very earliest years a fire a little further up from our Bute Cottages and I now know that some thatched cottages in Westoning Road burned down in October 1929 and although I don't remember it, an eighteenth century timber framed farm house in Westoning Road is shown in "Harlington In Camera" (Russell Preston) and this was demolished in 1928. Tabor Close is now on the site, part of the new development of Harlington.

But it is the cottages next to ours that stand out in my memory. They were built by Franklin's Coals with stables at the back for their beautiful hardworking Shire horses. I fell in love with these Gentle Giants, although I do recall that one of them was not quite so gentle as he might have been! He had a way of kicking out with his hind legs if anyone was near him. I believe his name was "Old Bob." The horses, two of them, both grey and white, were put into a field when they had finished work for the day in the summer months instead of going back to their stables. The field joined our back garden, a fence separating it from our land, but as I was always climbing things I managed to conquer that hurdle so that I could call the horses to me and reach out and stroke their huge, silky noses. This worried my mother so much for fear I would get hurt that wire netting had to be placed over the fence to stop me from climbing. In later years, my aunt and uncle, Mabel and Horace Asbury moved into the cottage and we moved down to Sundon Road. They bought land at the back of the vicarage and set up a big Nursery of tomatoes, cucumbers and flowers and kept livestock, including ducks because there was a lovely moat for the ducks to swim in. To get to their land they had to cross Franklin's field with the Shire horses in and I used to be with them quite often. The Shire horses were always docile, even Old Bob!

When I was very small I used to look out of the window of the back bedroom and on a fine day I could spot the people who played tennis on the lush green tennis court belonging to the old vicarage, now sadly no longer there. The then incumbent was the Revd. Arthur G. Hodgson, a very kindly clergyman who gave my father his full title when he spoke to him, John Albert.

Others just called him "Jim" or "Jimmy". The Revd Hodgson was responsible for the publication of a book, "The Great War 1914-1919; Men of Harlington (Harlington 1921)" Mrs. Hodgson was charming and she adored children.

Old Vicarage

On winter evenings in our Bute cottage home my parents, my sister and I gathered round the coal fire burning brightly in the old-fashioned living-room range. It took a lot of cleaning with black lead - and no doubt some spit-and-polish - and it must have been a filthy job, but most of the little cottages in those days had a similar cooking and heating arrangement and no one took any notice of the hard work involved.

Sometimes my father had a friend in to play chess with him. One of his friends was Percy Willey, the organist at Harlington Church at that time and uncle of Pearl who took over in later years and at this time of writing is still the organist at Harlington Church. I used to sit in a high chair by the table so that I could see the two men playing, fascinated by the pieces on the board.

My Gran and Grampy Lane lived next door to us by the side of Mr. and Mrs. Denton who lived in the Franklin's Coals house. Large, rosy-cheeked Gran wore a long black dress down to her ankles. Any poor snotty-nosed kids that found their way up Franklin's yard that was open to the roadway and peered through our fence she sent packing, especially the one that said to me when I was sucking an orange some alien words that sounded suspiciously like, 'Div me a bit of oos buddy owange, oo ickle budda'. He soon scampered off when Gran spoke severely to him and said, 'Shoo!' But I felt so sorry for the poor little lad that I would cheerfully have given him a bit of my orange and I didn't particularly want it after that.

On Sunday evenings we sat in Gran's cottage next door and supped her home-made wine. Cowslips and dandelions grew profusely in Harlington in those days. Dandelion wine in particular can be very potent, as I discovered in my adult years when I was married and my mother-in-law also made it. In childhood I was always given a very tiny glass of the cowslip, perhaps because it was more mellow and had a sweeter taste than the dandelion and it was always served up to me in that glass, which was quite antiquated. The glass was thick and well patterned and the handle was just large enough for me to grasp in my small fingers. It was kept in a black wooden three-corned cupboard hanging on Gran's sitting room wall. I would love to know what happened to it. If I had it now it would be greatly treasured. My husband Andy and I often laugh about that first time I sampled his mother's dandelion wine. I wasn't aware of its potency and swigged it down very quickly. Result? I was soon seeing Teddy Bears in little red skirts floating from the fireplace!

I was five years old when I started school. Two years later we moved down to the other end of the village, to Sundon Road which leads eventually to Sundon village and it was there that I met my little friend of very early childhood years. Her name was Joan and she lived next door to us. Together we would walk up the steep hill in our village that led to the centre of Harlington to the shops, the church and the school.

Chapter Three

Village School Days and Holidays

When I entered Harlington's Victorian school building, now the Parish Hall, on my way to a meeting in my adult years, I found myself looking around the rooms and reflecting upon how they used to be, not bare apart from chairs piled up or set around for gatherings. The "big room" as we had called it had housed my desk right at the back in the corner near the door that led to the boys' playground, this in the year 1933-34. I remembered the dividing door which, when open, was where the school dentist visited and I could almost smell that distinctive dental odour that made us cringe as we waited our turn to be attended to. So I thought on more pleasant things...

Pushed back, the dividing door naturally made our room much larger for end of term concerts, when we displayed to our parents and relatives our acting talents at that early age. It was the part of school days I loved most of all. My favourite play was "Winnie the Pooh," obviously because I was chosen to be "Tigger," and rolled my R's, representing a tiger-like noise, "Worra-Worra-Worra!"

For this I had to hide behind the school piano and jump out at the appropriate moment. That piano came in very useful for school plays. The angel Gabriel would glide from behind it in the Nativity play at Christmas. At Harlington Church there was always a Christmas tableau in which my father for a number of years portrayed Joseph. My mother, sister and I of course attended. But it was the image of the angel Gabriel that imprinted itself on my mind mostly. 'I want to be an ANGEL' I murmured. "Mmm!" was the only response I got from my mother, but it was loaded! However, if she thought I would never be an angel she was wrong, for the very next year I was chosen at school for the part of the angel Gabriel and I appeared from behind the piano in white with cardboard wings outspread across my back and uttered with great triumph those immortal words, "Fear not, for I bring you glad tidings of great joy ..."

After our own nativity at school, it was that glorious time to go home and enjoy our Christmas holidays. Off we went, carrying the special calendars we had made for our mothers. In our home Christmas was the best time of all the year, a time when relatives spent happy hours with us. Joint carol singing between the Methodist Church and the Church of St. Mary the Virgin took place from door to door, their old-fashioned lanterns lighting their way to the next house, for everywhere was in darkness apart from the lights shining from the windows. Street lighting didn't arrive in Harlington for many years after. My father had a rich tenor voice and he sang with the carol singers and also rang the Christmas bells. No more the old scenes though, for in 1989, many years later, the Round Tablers from nearby Toddington took over with their Christmas Sleigh and music relayed through their loudspeakers.

At our family feast on Christmas Day Gran and Grampy Lane arrived with my Auntie Mabel and Uncle Horace Asbury, although Uncle Horace had to hurry home at some point to stoke the boilers for the hot-house produce that was his livelihood, returning some time later. Grampy Lane always looked as though he belonged on the top of our Christmas cake. He would have made an excellent Father Christmas decoration! He was very short, with silvery hair, round, rosy cheeks and sparkling blue eyes and looked as though any minute he would break forth with a "Ho,ho,ho!" And he had a super Father Christmas white, pointed beard. Sitting in the glow of the fire on Christmas Day, not wishing to spoil the overall effect by switching on the electric light, we listened to Charles Dickens' "A Christmas Carol," usually read on the radio year after year. One year we were so immersed in the story that when it came to the part of the Spirit of Christmas Past we gasped as we heard a voice from the back of the room and turned to see a figure in white standing there. "I am the spirit of Christmas Past," it said in funereal tones. No-one moved at first, then someone switched on the light and there stood my mother, who had thrown off the sheet she was wearing and laughing, sat down and played us carols on her mandolin. She was a talented mandolinist and taught me to play also as I grew older.

During our Christmas holidays when the days were dark and drear outside, I used to curl up in a comfortable old armchair by the radio and listen entranced to the Children's Hour at tea-time, with "Uncle Mac" and "David" in the Toy Town series.

But most of all I loved the stories told by "Romany" of the countryside, when he was accompanied by his dog. Somewhat different from today's children, who play games on computers! (Romany's Caravan Returns and Out with Romany make excellent reading, although it is obvious by the publication lists of childrens' books today that something more exciting is now required!)

And then it was back to school to get on with our learning until the Easter break which brought with it Easter eggs and hot cross buns. They really were hot when they reached us from the baker's in a neighbouring village and were delivered to us at five o'clock in the morning. My sister and I would wake up very early to listen for him calling and hear our mother go downstairs to take in the buns she had ordered. Then, back upstairs she came to give us our treat, those buns all deliciously spread with melting butter.

In Harlington there was also bread given out to families and money to the children. Maundy bread and money it was called, from a charity for that purpose, but I don't remember much about it or when it stopped. On Ascension Day we all went to Harlington Church and on Empire Day, we sang with great gusto the Empire Day song, "Crocodiles live on the Niger, India has the stripey tiger..." And then we set about our early studies with thoughts of summer holidays in our minds, when for me picnics on the hills took priority. There were also Methodist Church fetes to look forward to and St. Mary's Church events held in the grounds of the Manor.

Those were golden days, with the spring-summer sun shining down on the school playgrounds and the field called Bury Orchard in which our school was built by the road. While waiting for the school whistle to blow to call us to our lessons we would run across to the village pond that we knew then as "The Dell," but is now known also as "Bacchus Pond." We would sit round the pond and make daisy chains, then make a quick dash across the field to the school when we heard the whistle blown. Daisies were not the only flora that grew by and near the pond. There were many more species in that vicinity and it would have made a great place for us to have held our nature study lessons in the summer, only we had to hold fast to the school rules and go back to the classroom for that.

That name Bacchus Pond for our Dell... It is known that a Bacchus Pond is shown on an 18th century map. This was a watering place for drovers' animals because of its purity. Could it be then, that the name Bacchus, God of Wine, has lent itself to our Pond through the purity of its waters? A lovely, romantic thought indeed, although there has been another explanation. More about the village Pond can be found on Harlington Local History Card Number Six, where flora and fauna also are listed in full detail.

Bacchus Pond

There was one part of Harlington school days, however, that I did not relish. It was going to the lavatory situated round the back of the school. Those lavatories of past years in the country left much to be desired. They were known as "earth closets" - although I have seen closets a lot "earthier!" Those are the kind where you just sit on the seat with a sheer drop into a bottomless pit below. One I remember well was in a wild part of Scotland and how terrified I was of falling down into the darksome depth, never to be seen again! Our school lavatories were of the bucket kind, with a ventilation at the back of the building wide enough for a small bird to squeeze through, as sometimes they did. I was always afraid that my bottom would get pecked as I sat there, so I often chose to wait until I went home, which of course wasn't good for me. Other lavatories in the village were also of the bucket kind found throughout the country in those days and in our village they were emptied about once a week. Sometimes they were so full that the buckets spilled in the road as they were carried to the horse-drawn wagon in which they were emptied. It was quite disgusting and very offensive. This wagon was called "the Muck Cart," although there is a word that would have suited it better! I was in my teenage years, I believe, when we had water closets laid on. Before that, I remember how embarrassed I was when I reached Luton for my studies and brought my town friends home. But those bucket days didn't stop them from visiting. They enjoyed every minute of their time in Harlington. It was a feature in some villages for earth lavatories to be two and sometimes three in one unit down the garden path. The part of Harlington called "The Rookery" was no exception. There would be two large seats for the adults to use and one small one for a child, or one large and one small and they could all be used at the same time. What could be called a family gathering!

Old Rookery

17

There were two teachers at school, one in the infants' room and the headmistress in the seniors'. The first one I remember was Mrs. Annie Giles, known to all in Harlington as "Teacher Annie." She was the infants' schoolteacher when I first arrived there. Very kindly, very motherly and very L-a-r-g-e! Her huge, comfortable frame would sit at the piano where she would thump away with heavy hands on the keys, her foot beating time as she would give us our start to sing - "One-and-two-and-three-and". As she sat there, we could see her long directoire bloomers stretched well down over her knees. We all loved her. But she wasn't there long in my infancy before she left and was replaced by Miss Irene Robinson from Maulden.

Miss Robinson was well built and tall, quite a handsome young woman with jet black hair and an extremely pleasant manner. We had a very happy time under her reign in the infants' room. On Friday afternoons she would be joined by her sister, Miss Dorothy Robinson, also from Maulden. Dorothy was a teacher, too, but at that time she was "Resting" from her career. Later, she became the schoolteacher at Millbrook village school. When she visited us on Friday afternoons she brought with her a large bag of sweets which were handed round our classroom and she told us lovely childrens stories. She was a delightful person. Dorothy wore long, dangly earrings and was very slim, while Irene had a buxom figure emphasised by a red and yellow tartan skirt and a bright yellow jumper. It was a bit startling, but it set off her ample bosom and dynamic personality.

Dorothy and Irene Robinson's brother, Harry Robinson, was Clerk to the Council of Ampthill District (now Mid Beds District Council) and Registrar of births, marriages and deaths. There is a part of Harlington now named after him, Robinson Crescent, where elderly people's Council bungalows have been built. He was also a local Methodist Preacher. A very happy co-incidence for me is that after my marriage my husband Andy and I went to live in Maulden and I met again the two Robinson sisters, long since retired from their teaching days and we became good friends.

The headmistress at Harlington school was Miss Minnie Coleman. Small, neat and thin, her spindly legs looked as though they would break in half and she always wore high heeled brown shoes with a strap across her instep and pointed toes, a fashion that has surely returned time and again during this present age. Her eyes were dark brown set in a face with a sallow skin and you knew it wouldn't be wise to give her any cheek, although one boy did and she could do nothing with him. In fact, she seemed half afraid of him, which wasn't surprising for he was huge and very strong and came from a very rough, tough family and he even punched Miss Coleman if she reprimanded him. But one day he met his match ...

Going home from school, I was followed by this boy who was known as the school bully. He caught up with me outside "The Carpenters Arms," where I turned and confronted him. I was only tiny and he towered above me and started knocking me about, so I brought up my little foot and kicked him where it hurt most for a boy. I felled him in one and he lay on the ground crying for mercy. I didn't know until then that we were being watched by our dairyman, Mr. Steve Smith, who was looking out of the pub window and getting ready to rescue me. With a burst of laughter he strode from the pub, said, 'Well done, little 'un. Come on, get in my van and I'll take you home.' By this time Big Bully Boy had risen to his feet and started for his own home, holding his private parts and bawling his head off. On reaching my home Mr Smith handed me over to my mother and told her, 'Your kid's got guts. She can stand up for herself.' When mother told Miss Coleman about the incident, my headmistress said that at last the big, bad boy had got his "desserts" and if she couldn't manage him in class she'd call on little Edna Lane to settle him. I never heard of the school bully trying anything on after that, though.

Miss Coleman lived in the school house opposite the school with her friend, Miss Lichfield, who was her housekeeper and cook. Miss Lichfield was short and dumpy and always ready to give us comfort if we hurt ourselves in the school playground and to make our wounds better when we were sent across to her. She died while living at Harlington with Miss Coleman who, on her retirement left to live in Harrold, north Bedfordshire.

School House

Revd. G.A. Butler had been the founder of my old school in 1859, a National (church) School. The School house is said to most probably be standing on the site of the old parsonage, which was the one before the Old Vicarage opposite the church that I remember in my childhood days. The house was built in 1876. My father told me about his schoolmaster who had lived there. He was Mr. Charles Apthorpe. It has been written that he was very popular, and he surely had a lot to contend with in trying to keep my father and his school pals in order, so maybe it's quite understandable that he must have lost patience with them sometimes. When that happened, said my father, he would bring in his wife to sit on them while he put them across his knee and gave them a dose of the cane. By the photos I have seen, Mrs. Apthorpe, who was the infants' teacher, was of good proportions. But I'm sure those naughty boys must have deserved what they got! I It is known that Mr. Apthorpe was a keen and excellent gardener and taught his boys to be the same. It must have rubbed off with good effect, for in his adult years my father also followed in his wake, and had a commendable garden of flowers and vegetables. Mr. Apthorpe was also the Church Organist and Choirmaster in my father's day. It is comforting to see the old school building still standing, although it is no longer used for school purposes, the pupils now being educated first at Harlington Lower School (five to nine years); then Parkfields Middle School (nine to thirteen) at Toddington; and then back to Harlington Upper School (thirteen to eighteen).

Chapter Four

Methodist Memories

Wesleyan Methodism in Harlington has quite a colourful background. It has known three chapels and it is also said that there was primarily a Methodist Meeting House in some part of the village, perhaps Chapel Yard. An early one in Sundon Road dated 1836 became residential homes when another chapel was built in 1883. In my time in Harlington my mother's cousin, Lily Dudley and her husband lived in one of the little homes. I often visited her there. The yellow brick shell has now been incorporated into a new residence and as such can be seen opposite "The Old Sun." The second chapel became known as the Old Chapel when the third one called the New Chapel was built in 1928. A lady I knew so well laid the foundation stone to this new chapel built in neo-Gothic style. She was called "Aunt Patti." A hall was added at a much later date, with a new porch, toilet and store room built in 1983, making it suitable for all events. On 26th April 1998 a special celebration service was held and a commemorative photographic display illustrating the colourful history of Methodism in Harlington.

As a child I attended the Methodist Church Sunday School in the Old Chapel. My father was a devout member of the Church of England. My mother, a Wesleyan Methodist, demanded of my older sister and me that we attended her own church in our early years. But as those years went by, although my sister continued in Methodism, I turned towards my father's church, changing my denomination at the age of nineteen.

Earliest Chapel

Old Chapel

Apart from Sunday School the Old Chapel was also used for Christian Endeavour meetings, Youth Club, old film shows and some entertaining concerts in which my mother and I took part with our mandolins. During the Second World War years, on the arrival of evacuees from Walthamstow it was used as their week-day school by some of them. The Sunday School scholars also took part in the Sunday School Eisteddfod held in Bedford. My mother coached us for elocution. I think that must have been when my interest in theatre studies really took off, although it didn't come to fruition until years later.

My parents had great respect for each other's denominations, dad supporting mother in her chapel activities and mother doing the same for him at church. It made for a happy family life. In my time at the Methodist Church the preachers came from the Dunstable circuit. Sunday School was made more than usually enjoyable by our rather ancient Superintendent Mr. Cleaver when he recounted his tales of his youth in his own inimitable style, especially when he announced to us that 'Miss Gazely is hat the horgin this mornin.' That "horgin" which, I believe was actually a harmonium, appeared to be even more ancient than our quaint old Super. Sometimes Miss Kitty Chambers played the "horgin" for us and for many years now she has been one of the organists at the New Chapel. At the time of writing she is still playing in that capacity. Mr. Alfred Denton who worked in the office of Franklin's Coals near the station, shared Sunday School duties with Mr. Cleaver. He was a very good-living and kindly Man.

In the Old Chapel the Ladies' Bright Hour started in the early 1920s as a sewing class, but later changed to a meeting with speakers, prayers and readings. My mother became a member. Aunt Patti usually led the prayers. A rare character, she was born in the neighbouring village of Westoning in 1870 and

New Chapel

Patti Stone

came to live in Harlington while she was still a baby. When she died at the age of 95 in her own home on 18th March 1966 she left a large family of children, grandchildren and great-grand-children, the last one being born about the date of her death. As a girl I remember her wearing long, black old-fashioned clothes and what I can only describe as a po-shaped black hat. Aunt Patti, when she was a child, was one of many children in villages who worked in straw plait.

One day when the old combustion stove had been lit in preparation for the Ladies' Bright Hour held every Thursday in the Old Chapel, the roof caught fire due to the old stove pipes overheating. This was in December 1952. It is a story that lives on through the years, but I was told it first by my mother. The Ladies' Bright Hour has come a long way since those days of the sewing class, which Aunt Patti's grand-daughter, Mrs. Ruby Hillyard remembers attending with her when Ruby was a child. After its closure as a church, the Old Chapel was used as business premises and in very recent times was put up for sale as a private residence.

In the New Chapel Sunday School anniversaries were held once a year when the children sang and recited religious pieces in the afternoon and the Chapel choir gave full voice in the evening. Then came summer, bringing with it great antici-pation, a coach ride to Wicksteed Park, Kettering with its water shute making us shriek with delight as we got disgustingly wet and all the other things for kids to enjoy, followed by a scrump-tious tea in the restaurant. And then there was the statue of Mr. Wicksteed's little dog Jerry and the poignant story he wrote in his book which mother bought me one year before we left. I couldn't wait to get home before starting to read it and as it was so sad I ended up in tears for most of the journey. For those who don't know, it tells of how "Grampa" Wicksteed, as he called himself, went shooting rabbits with his very much loved little dog, but during the process he shot the little fellow by mistake, thinking it was a rabbit leaping about some distance from him in the long grass. Heartbroken, he had the statue erected in the Park. Although longer journeys took us to the seaside, usually Clacton or Southend, I think I can honestly say that Kettering and Wicksteed Park were our favourite outings.

Today, Wicksteed Park which was opened in 1921, is very different from how it was in my Sunday School outing days. I don't know what "Grampa" Wicksteed would say if he could see it now with its added leisure section of Roller Coaster, Ferris Wheel, Chairoplanes and many other modern attractions. This true, gentle country man with a love for the simple things of life might be rather sad, I feel. And that restaurant where we used to enjoy our Sunday School teas with such relish - well, what a choice of eating places now! There's the Oak Tree Takeaway, Hexagon Restaurant, Kandy Kabin Vendodrome... And I'm sure that today's child finds it exciting and a great delight for a day's outing. For myself, a child of yesteryear, I find it soothing to know that little Jerry's statue can still be seen in the Rose Garden where it has always been, although it's rather the worse for wear, I'm sorry to say! This in millennium year, 2000.

A little note of extra interest... The mother of a friend of mine, a lady born and bred in Kettering but who in her later years came to live in Harlington, told the story to her daughter of how "Grampa" Wicksteed used to ride through Kettering in his horse-drawn carriage and throw sixpences (those little silver coins long extinct in our country) to the children.

******

27

Grampa's Memorial Poem to Jerry:

Little Brown Dog you played your part
In a Dream that came from your Master's heart
With the building of bridges and fording of streams
In the Park that arose from your Master's dreams.

No wonder I howled my eyes out all the way home from our Sunday School outing!

Chapter Five

Picnic on the hills

'No, you can't go for your picnic until that nice boy arrives from Windsor'.

My mother's voice sounded loud and clear as she turned to confront the children thronging round her in our garden. We had gathered to ask, When, when PLEASE would the annual outing be taking place? It wasn't the only picnic we had each year, but It was the BIG ONE, a super event to be remembered throughout the winter months and to be looked forward to again for the following year. Those picnics started when I was about ten and they were shared with three boys, one other girl and two little ones who lived nearby. "Little Joan" as she was called because she was much smaller than I was, although only a year younger, was my friend who lived next door. We played together, rambled over the surrounding fields together, went blackberrying and crab-appling for my mother to make delicious blackberry and crab-apple jelly and took visits "down the Rec" (Recreation ground where there were TWO WONDERFUL SWINGS and nothing else!) Today, houses are standing in the part near the old allotments. They and the Rec. are no more. Instead the houses built became the residential area now known as Goswell End. We spent our Saturday pence together at the post office that was also a shop. One penny piece bought a stick of liquorice and some vinegar flats, sweets we adored. Joan and I were the two oldest of the picnic children. My cousin Ken and his friend Dennis were the two boys in our group and they just couldn't wait for "that nice boy from Windsor" to arrive and stay with his auntie who lived next door to cousin Ken and opposite Joan and me. Peter was several years older than the rest of us. But when the war came, it broke up Peter's rendezvous with us and he was spirited away, never to return. After he died at a rather early age, I met the girl he married and we became friends, a friendship that has lasted.

And so to those picnics. Outside my parents' house we congregated. One of the grown-ups had a pram in which the teenies sat and rode in comfort - well, as comfortable as it could be for them, for, although they sat on the hood side, the other side of the pram was packed solid with our picnic equipment. There were cooking pots, a huge frying pan and groceries galore. We certainly weren't going to be hungry on our picnic!

Happiness abounded as we skipped and danced along, the boys and just two girls, while Peter from Windsor played his mouth organ. Laughter rang as we progressed along the dusty road that led to Markham Hills with their neighbours, the Clappers, a bit further along. The road was long and fairly straight and all the time we could see those inviting hills, seemingly beckoning us on. We passed Wood Farm, partly Georgian and partly of an earlier period, home of the Lee family. Before the Lee family moved in a family by name of Kent lived there. Margaret, one of the girls, was a friend of my sister and in their season at the farm the long stretch of grassland going down to the road was covered in snowdrops -just a mass of white. A walnut tree had an inviting swing on it for the young family and their friends. On the opposite side of the road was a pleasant looking bungalow with a tennis court. The bungalow has since been turned into a house and next to it another bungalow has been built.

Wood Farm

Further down, opposite the cow-shed entrance, was an old but solid looking hut. We wondered what mystery lay in its darkened depth. Joan's mum enlightened us. 'That's where old Doddun lives,' she said. 'He's lived there a long time. He's very clean and kind and he works on the farm.' In later days Joan and I were to meet old Doddun, when Joan's Mum sent food to him and we delivered It. There he would sit by a smoky fire, with the pungent smell of his baccy in his pipe almost choking us. He was very old and wrinkled and he had very kind, brilliant blue eyes. A dear old man. When Doddun died, he was replaced by another, very similar old boy named Darby. Indeed a story to stir children's imagination. Just past Doddun's hut were some beehives. Although they were close by the road, they didn't bother passers by. They belonged to one of the much older members of the Kent family.

Doddun's Hut

Continuing on our way down the long, straight road, we passed Dyers Hall, set back from the road. It is now no longer there. An Army firing range put paid to it during their practice days of the Second World War. I was not in Harlington when this happened, having been called up for war service, but before this, when I was a cub reporter on the then local newspaper group, Home Counties Newspapers Limited, I was detailed by my editor to visit Dyers Hall and interview some old folk who had been evacuated to there. They were evacuated again, else-where so they would be safe from the Army firing range. At ten years of age I was hardly aware of the existence of Dyers Hall, this in the days of our picnics! The only thing that concerned me was reaching those enticing hills.

The end of the road forked to Sundon village, up a steep hill on the right, while to the left in the corner was a hidden spring, keeping a watercress bed flourishing. This was the beginning of the narrow road that led round "The Bottoms" taking people along the lower east end of Harlington and bringing them out eventually at the bottom of Abbot's Hill and on the road to Sharpenhoe and Barton-le-Clay, or turning left, up the hill and back into Harlington. But our picnic party branched off long before reaching Abbot's Hill, passing through a wide gate that was always open on the right. This took us through a field and on to a cart track that led to a farm right at the bottom of "Markham Hills."

Mrs. Piggot and her daughter, Dorothy, lived at the farm. They were friendly and obliged us with eggs and milk to take up the hills for our picnic, and anything else we required. There was a small pond where ducks swam, hens roamed free - and a goose or two that let us know in no uncertain terms not to get too close to their property. This was a very relaxed farm. I deem it sad that it had to be sacrificed through the firing range in Harlington during World War Two and the Piggots had to vacate their home which was blown to pieces. I visited the spot years after. There was just an empty space where the farm had been. But at this time of writing, the pond is still there. While shopping in Luton in my adult years I met up again with Dorothy Piggot. I had often wondered what had happened to her. She enlightened me. She had joined the A.T.S. (Auxiliary Territorial Service, long since disbanded) and had become a driver. Miss Piggot was tall and well built and straight as a rod and was quite a handsome woman, with rosy cheeks. She rode a beautiful chestnut mare which she sat magnificently, taking it up to Harlington village most days. She was the only horse rider we ever saw apart from our doctor from the neighbouring village of Toddington, Dr. Ralph Fawcett, who had been a Boer War Army Field Surgeon. He rode round the villages attending his patients long before he used a car to do so. A character indeed, with his brilliant blue eyes, his whiskers thick and curled up at the ends reminiscent of Boer War days, striding along when not riding in his well shone brown leather leggings. There were very few cars on the road then, so horse riders were quite safe.

There was a steep climb to the top of the grass hill for our picnic. Goodness knows how we managed to get there well laden with our goodies, pram, pots and pans, but we did. After all, there were enough of us to help with everything and the boys were strong, especially Peter, who was tall and muscular. Right at the top was a background of fir trees, forming a wonderful shelter from the wind that might blow on us as we enjoyed our camp fire. It was because of those fir trees that the hills were commonly called "The Firs." Other trees of course grew there, but it was from the firs that the air was so heaven-scented, relaxing us and adding to our enjoyment. From the hilltop there was a steep bank down where hazel bushes were clustered and after we had had our food - sizzling sausages, potatoes cooked on the camp fire - we, the children, would clamber down the slopes and if some of the hazelnuts were ripe enough, we would gather them.

But first of all we had our orders from the adults, to "go and fill the containers down at the spring." That spring was quite a distance from our camp and to walk back from it with our full water containers was quite a task. As I travel from Barton on my way to Luton now, so many years later, I see the place in the shadows across the bottom part of that countryside from "Markham Hills" where our group of kids filled those water containers. So many people pass that way and don't even know of its existence. To me, it is "special."

It was difficult to find a flat piece of land on which to play cricket, but we did. We didn't play the game strictly to rule, but it was fun and even the large jolly lady, one of the Mums, joined in and her capers caused great mirth amongst us!

The boys climbed trees. Of course they did! Perhaps showing off because two girls were present. There was a huge, inviting oak tree near the camp and Peter gave us an example of his prowess by climbing to its tallest region, almost disappearing amongst its leafy height. When he came down again I thought "That really was something. But boys aren't going to beat me!" So I climbed.... and climbed .... and climbed. Well, it was one thing going up, but it was another thing trying to get down and when I stupidly looked at the ground I cried out and quaked. Peter was up the tree in a flash. Was I glad I had my shorts on and not a dress. But always a young gentleman, Peter averted his eyes from the tops of my legs and just murmured with an amused smile, 'Silly kid!' Then he gently led me down the tree. Ever after he was my girlhood hero.

Time to go home and we packed our pots and pans and braced ourselves for the long walk down the steep hill, first calling at Piggot's farm to say 'Thank you and goodbye.' Peter's mouth organ was put into action again and the music echoed in the summer air and we sang and danced and skipped and laughed our way up the cart track, along the dusty narrow road to the watercress bed, where we turned right to Harlington.

Healthily tired, little Joan and I leaned out of our bedroom windows - the houses were semi-detached - to say our last good nights to one another. Then to bed. But first I glanced towards the hills and my imagination took off into realms far distant before I drifted into sleep. It has been said that highwaymen had their hiding places up in those hills many years past. What a place of action that part of the Bedfordshire countryside has been!

Many years later, after linking up with Harlington again through my visit to the John Bunyan display at Harlington Church, I received a pamphlet regarding the Parish Paths Partnership, known as P3, a Countryside Initiative. This is a National scheme aiming to give encouragement to local people to get involved in the management of rights of way within their respective parishes. It is supported and financed by the County Council. From Harlington's Footpath Guide No.1. I learned that "The Bottoms" of my childhood is called Harlington Vale. Well, it IS at the lowest east end of the village, the main part of which of course stands on a hill. "The Bottoms" road along which we walked to our picnic on the hills was once known as "Hoardfield Lane." There was once an old hamlet at the east end. This interesting pamphlet obtained from the parish clerk, Harlington Parish Council, tells of much more regarding the path where my childhood steps once trod.

Chapter Six

Along The Wick Herne Way.

As I pass down Sundon Road, Harlington, at the end of the village as I often do today, I do not always see what in reality lies before me - a turning to the right with modern houses stretching on towards the railway bridge and round a corner. Quite a vast expanse now called Park Leys, the building of which was begun in or round-about 1976. Instead, the door marked "Yesterday" opens in my mind and I step through to feast on many happy childhood-girlhood memories.

The stile, where Joan and I would sit and watch the world go by and eat our sticks of liquorice or whatever we had bought from the post office-sweet shop with our small weekly allowance of pocket money, has a replacement of bricks and mortar. In fact, my own cousin's bungalow is somewhere round about that spot. It was called "the Lane stile" leading into the "Lane field," (nothing to do with my own family name, Lane). A long, narrow path led down to another field on the right with a thick blackberry hedge dividing it off from my great-aunt's garden. In the field stood a giant oak tree of much more magnificence than the John Bunyan one that we climbed in a different part of Harlington. It was a favourite spot of ours for sheltering from the hot sun in the summer. Along the hedgerows separating the field from the road the sweet, soft perfume of violets wafted across to us. They grew in profusion, both white and purple.

Joan and I, with our companions, often set off on rambles across the Lane field. Peter from Windsor would be in tow while visiting Harlington during the summer months in his school holidays. Passing through a gate to the next field, we came to the railway and a railway bridge right at the bottom. Sometimes farm cattle had congregated under the bridge from the field the other side and we had to send them off by shouting and waving of arms (the boys were very good at that!)

The railway was part of our childhood scene and we had no memories of how that scene had been before the railway was built, but it is said there was a farm house the other side of the bridge not far from a pond. The pond, now dried up, was and is known as "Farm Pond." As children we would gather round the pond and throw stones into it to see who could throw the furthest distance. It was almost always full of water then. The old farm was pulled down, I am told, to make way for the building of the railway, the Midland main line to London.

Harlington station (Harlington for Toddington), was opened in 1868. The famous cricketer, W.G. Grace is said to have stopped off at Harlington station when he played cricket in our neighbouring village, Toddington. My father, an enthusiastic cricketer, was for ever telling me this! But a more up to the minute note of interest is surely the naming of a new Thameslink locomotive 319030. The name? "Harlington Festival." The ceremony in 1994 was attended by more than three hundred people on Harlington station, platform number three. First, the Revd Steve Williams, vicar of Harlington Parish Church, St. Mary the Virgin, blessed the train and named it, then Thameslink managing director Jim Collins received a commemorative off cut from John Bunyan's Oak presented to him by John McFadden. Mr. McFadden was project manager for the electrifying of the Bedford-London services. This eventful occasion in 1994, so many years on from my childhood, took place when Harlington held its second Harlington Festival (we didn't have such things in my early days) and Harlington was the first of Thameslink's Stations to have a class 319 locomotive named in its honour. My link with Harlington had not been renewed when the Thameslink ceremony happened, so I was not among those attending it. These details appeared in an excellent report by Mr. Bob Hedley in the Harlington village magazine, Contact, October 1994 and which Mr. Hedley has kindly given me permission to use. Mr Hedley's main family connection is with ship building, but his great-great grandfather, William Hedley invented the steam locomotive the "Puffing Billy," first used at Wyland Colliery and later connected with George Stephenson.

The Midland railway and the opening of Harlington railway station on 13th July 1868 gave extra employment to the village and surrounding area. Thus it was that a row of railway cottages was built for Midland Railway employees down at the bottom end of one of the oldest roads in Harlington, namely Station Road, (previously Ampthill Street). It was in the first of these cottages that my aunt and uncle, Mabel and Horace Asbury, lived before moving into the Bute Cottage in Westoning Road where I was born.

Railway Station

39

Railway Cottages

In our days of childhood it was a great thrill to watch the steam trains approaching along the old line and especially when the "Flying Scotsman" was due we congregated to watch it pass - so quickly that it was gone in a flash. A Railway Exhibition held in Harlington Methodist Hall each year has been of extreme interest and has drawn people from the village and surrounding areas.

Back to childhood, leaving Farm Pond in the shelter of its graceful trees, our little group of children made its way from the vicinity of the railway and up the sloping field to one of our favourite haunts where many rabbits scampered about, appearing and disappearing down their warren. We called this place "Weak Earn," but I now know it by its correct name, "Wick Herne." This part of countryside is where changing scenes have drastically taken their toll, brought about by a series of supervised archaeological digs among other things. Finds are now deposited in Luton Museum and Art Gallery (see Archaeological Journals) and it is now not a place for children to spend their happy hours. But today's children find more sophisticated ways of spending their time other than watching little rabbits with their bobbing tails scampering about!

For us it was heaven, with no adults to disturb us. There was an old, gnarled crab-apple tree, but it was not too old to bear fruit. Unfortunately, when Peter was with us in August, the crab-apples were not ready for gathering, but he wasn't to know that, being a "towny," and we had to warn him to "keep his mitts off" or he would regret it! When the crab-apples WERE ripe was after Peter had gone home to Windsor. But Peter succumbed to temptation, much to his cost, for on reaching his auntie's house where he stayed for his summer holidays he had to keep running along the garden path to the lavatory. The next day, Peter was so poorly with stomach ache that his auntie kept him in bed, which was where he was when we called for him to go out with us. And who got the blame? I did, because, his auntie said, 'You ought to have known better, Edna, than to have let him eat all those blackberries. After all, you are older than the others.' Little did she know it wasn't just BLACKBERRIES he had eaten. What would she have said if she had known he had been sampling unripe CRAB-APPLES! I hadn't ever the heart to tell Peter about the baskets of crab-apples we gathered a bit later in the season and the late blackberries to go with them for my mother to make lovely blackberry and crab-apple jelly which we ate with clotted cream ordered from our dairyman, Mr. Steve Smith, just up the road. With her home-made scones they were delicious. Poor Peter would have cried out with longing. He loved my mother's cooking!

We move on in time, but those days of delightful memories linger with us, even though the countryside is fast disappearing beneath modern developments. Toddington Motorway Services is just over from where our childhood ramblings were. But we must admit the railway - the trains, especially the electrified ones and the opening of Harlington station is to our overall advantage, and we can't have everything.

Chapter Seven

Walking to Granny's

She was Joan's Granny, but she was known to many others through the village as "Granny Harris." Very tall, very thin, very wrinkled was she, with piercing black eyes and very old. Upright as a rod, she walked most days come wind, come weather, across the fields from the other end of the village to Joan's parents' house at the bottom of Sundon Road, Harlington. She looked so stern, as indeed she could be and she was very outspoken and forthright, which didn't suit some people. But she could also be very kind. A discerning old lady who didn't miss a thing of what was happening around her. She had a very old, plump black Field spaniel called Nell who accompanied her everywhere and when Nell died at a great age her son, Joan's Uncle Slimmy, brought home another dog to keep her company. The second was a little black and white terrier type named Jumbo. Joan and I loved the dogs. Neither of us had a pet of our own at that time. Uncle Slimmy, whose name was George, was very kind. During our school holidays from an early age Joan and I walked to Granny's. Our walk began by Sunnymede Villas on the opposite side of the road from where we lived. Our two houses and the villas marked the end of the village in those days, apart from Wood Farm and the bungalow round the corner. Now the village continues with Park Leys next to Sunnymede Villas and on the opposite side of the road some new houses, part of the new development of Harlington. Before this, Harlington was a typical English village, with cottages in abundance, a goodly number of which have disappeared. Right next to our own homes, however, were and still are four very nice old cottages which have been attractively improved during the latter years and stand out prominently with their white walls. Once upon a time in my memory an old lady named Fleur lived in the first one next to our house. She looked a bit weird with her fly-away straight grey hair, no teeth and old but very clean clothes. Her little cottage was spotless, too, and she was a very kind lady. Strange, maybe, that old Fleur had a very elegant niece who was a mannequin in London and who visited her aunt at week-ends!

Sunnymede Villas

At one time Joan's Granny used to live in one of a row of cottages next to the four white cottages, but the row of little homes was demolished and Granny went to live in a lovely olde-worlde homestead called "Mulberry Cottage" at the other side of the village, which was the destination of our walk. One of the little group of demolished cottages had included an open hall house dating from c1500. This was demolished in 1979. It does seem rather sad that such an ancient house should have had to go, but there are many like homes throughout the countryside that have received the same fate.

Next came my Great-aunt May and Uncle Jack's picturesque old cottage. Memories galore come flooding back here, especially of those Harlington school days when I used to pop in on the way home from school to see if they wanted anything from the village shop. Even if they didn't, I knew I would get some pocket money given me! Great-aunt May was my mother's aunt and a sister of my Grandma Lucy. Her home is still standing, but of course with different residents now and I have learned so much more about it from them than my Great-aunt could ever have told me. It is so old and interesting that I feel it deserves special recognition but for the time being I will just tell how Great-aunt May would most days be leaning over the gate to have a cheerful word with those who passed by. Very generously built, with a beaming rosy face, she would love to greet the children with a happy smile. Years later, after she and Uncle Jack were no longer with us, her home, "Rose Cottage," acquired a new name. Anyone who now looks for "Rose Cottage" under that name would not find it.

Next to Great-aunt May's cottage was the dairy where we bought milk and eggs, standing near the road further down the driveway from the old house, "Lavender Cottage," where Mr. Steve Smith, our dairyman lived.

Nothing much is known today of a row of very old interesting looking half-timbered cottages still standing, veering off from the road next to our dairyman's home, but I recall a Miss Slade, retired school mistress (not connected to a future Mrs Slade, schoolmistress at Harlington School.) Miss Slade lived in the first of these cottages. She was very kind to two little girls who were wartime evacuees billeted on her later on.

Mr. and Mrs. Guess, a dear old couple, lived in a cottage, one of two or three timber-framed and standing directly at the side of the road. They were opposite the public house now known as "The Old Sun." These cottages, eighteenth century, are no longer there. I well remember, though, the old couple standing at their door opening straight on to the road and having a friendly chat with passers by as Great-aunt May did and many other old people in those days. It was the only highlight of their day, no doubt, for they had no transport to take them anywhere, couldn't get to the station or 'bus stop' when they were really old and there was no television. Just a very old-fashioned battery wireless set, batteries bought at Ray Walton's garage just across the road from Steve Smith's.

Ray had a very interesting collection of old vehicles including motorbikes, photographs of which are now in the family album owned by his son, Roy who lives In Scotland. A photo in the book, "Old Harlington in Camera (2)" compiled by Russell Preston and Stephen Castle, shows a 1928 Dennis Fire Brigade engine at Walton's garage 1964, being prepared for an Open Day at Shuttleworth Museum, Old Warden. A photo in Harlington Village Magazine, "Contact" May 1998, shows the engine and states that it was originally from Luton Fire Brigade and then was part of the fleet of Skefko Ball Bearing Company. Ray Walton's garage was demolished in the 1980's so that Strafford Close could be constructed during the development of Harlington.

Continuing our walk, Joan and I passed one of the three public houses in the village, "The Old Sun" already mentioned, at the bottom of the hill leading up to the centre of Harlington. It was then called "The Rising Sun," half-timbered and dating back to the 17th Century. In later years the pub was altered and its frontage changed. It became "The Sun Inn," but it has since had its third change of name. It is said to be the oldest of the

45

three public houses in the village. The others are "The Carpenters Arms" at the top of the hill and "The Harlington Arms" in Station Road, now a private residence. Not bad for a village to have a pub at the foot of the hill and another at the top - a tipple before you start your journey and a top-up at the end.

The Old Sun

Through my early years up to the time of my marriage, I remember three of the landlords. Arthur Giles stands out because he had two children, a boy named Basil of about my own age and Doreen, who was in my sister's age group. They may have moved to Luton, for it was there that I bumped into Doreen again in my adult years. Mr. Maidment was a later landlord. I believe he and his wife with their two grown up sons came from London. The sons cut a dash in the village with their snazzy sports car, taking certain young village maidens "for rides!". The last landlord I remember was there at the time of my marriage. He was Horace Hartop. He and his wife left with their son to take over "The Blackbirds" at Flitwick, where he died.

In 1926 J.W. Green of Luton were "The Old Sun's" brewers. The lady of Harlington Manor when I was young was J.W. Green's daughter, Mrs. Gertrude Tabor, wife of Major Sydney Tabor. I came to know her very well in later years when in my cub reporting days for Home Counties Newspapers Ltd I wrote about her antiques. Ever after she referred to me as "My young friend, Edna Lane." After "The Old Sun" Joan and I came to the old and new Methodist Churches standing opposite each other, the new one next door to the public house. A bit daunting perhaps for Methodists, remembering their rules on abstinence from alcohol!

Next to the Old Chapel two cottages still exist. They are Sundown Cottages. In one of them there once lived a baker who allowed the Chapel worshippers to put their Sunday meat in his oven to help cook it while they attended the service. It was quite a common occurrence. I have read of other villages where this was done.

Brian Letting, an Old Harlingtonian like myself, shares with me the memory of his Aunt Lou and her husband giving sanction for a doctor to hold surgery in their cottage, one of the aforementioned. The doctor was Michael O'Donnell from Barton-le-Clay who became my own doctor after my marriage. Later, the surgery was moved a little further up the road to a house called "Westholme" where one of the Methodist Church organists lived. I remember her as Mrs. Rowley, but she remarried on the death of her husband and became Mrs. Bracy.

Dr. Jim O'Donnell, Michael's brother from Sundon Park, took over and had other partners with him. I don't know when Dr. Jim O'Donnell retired, but there are now at this point in time several doctors in partnership who have a surgery at Harlington, the old surgery having moved from Mrs. Bracy's home "Westholme" to Westoning Road and Dr. Michael O'Donnell's son, Patrick (nephew of Dr. Jim O'Donnell) is one of them. It was Mrs. Bracy, by then a grand old lady in her eighties, who opened it in 1987. Harlington at last has its own special doctor's surgery!

Our family doctor, Ralph Fawcett from Toddington, was the opposite number of the O'Donnells. He was the one who rode around the village on horseback - said it was good exercise - and in his gruff, stern voice would say, on entering the patient's house, 'And how are you, y'poor thing?' Then he would give a cheeky chuckle.

Adjoining "Westholme" was the Old Smithy's forge by an overhanging tree. When I was young I thought it must have been the Village Smithy of the old poem, "Under the Spreading Chestnut tree the Village Smithy stands," until I was old enough to realise I had got the wrong tree! Mr. Arthur Smith from Sundon village was at the Smithy for many years. Every weekday morning he would cycle down the steep hill to Harlington to his work at the Old Forge. As there were plenty of cart horses still in those days - tractors didn't do ALL the work - he was kept busy with shoe-ing and other tasks performed at his forge which was at the brow of the hill at Harlington. Some of the village boys took great delight in holding the horses' heads for him while he worked. Henry Wadsworth Longfellow knew his subject when he wrote:

> And children coming home from school
> Look in at the open door;
> They love to see the flaming forge
> And hear the bellows roar,
> And catch the burning sparks that fly
> Like chaff from a threshing floor.

Miss Hetty Stansfield of Harlington was a schoolteacher at Sundon, so every morning she walked the long distance UP the steep hill to that village and every evening she walked back DOWN to Harlington. Was it a co-incidence that one day after the death of his first wife who was an invalid, Miss Stansfield and Mr. Smith married? Did romance blossom on the hill? After his retirement Mr. Smith and his second wife Hetty moved to Ampthill, where they lived comfortably for a long time. It was in Ampthill when I reached my later years that I met Hetty again after knowing her in my village of Harlington when I was a girl.

Opposite "Westholme" and the Old Forge was a peaceful-looking old farm house called "Hillside" with apple trees hanging over the wall to the road. Apple scrumping was rife, for the apple trees were just inside the gate and, although Joan and I didn't venture through it, the boys of the village did. The name of the people who lived there was Gedge. Their son, John, who was about fifteen when we knew him, must have thought Joan and I were dear little girls, because he always climbed an apple tree, picked some apples and threw them down to us. After the Gedge family, members of the very old Harlington farming family of Giles moved in and one branch or another of them has lived there throughout the years.

Next to the Old Forge Joan and I would take a sharp turning right and - THERE IT WAS! The post office where we bought our sweets, well, most of the time, but if they hadn't got what we wanted we had to go to the next shop on the Square, known as "Jimmy's." But we weren't often disappointed at the post office. I would point out that we weren't allowed money for sweets EVERY day - our parents couldn't afford it, as well as it not being good for our teeth, and often we had to earn our sweet money so as to learn to appreciate it. As my mother used to say, 'Money doesn't grow on trees!'

Miss Nellie Snoxall ran the post office itself, while her sister, Mrs. Mabel Hill, kept the sweet shop. Two good looking silver-haired ladies who always had a cheerful word for everyone, particularly for the children. Mrs. Hill would lean over the counter and say to Joan and me with a kindly smile, 'And what would you like then, Duckies?' As though she didn't know! Sherbet Dabs, Licquorice Sticks and those sharp little Vinegar Flats. Hardly ever Chocolate, because it was dearer and we got more for our money with the other things.

The post office sisters had two beautiful white Persian cats with blue eyes. When we went into the post office we always found one or the other of them sitting on the counter. We were fascinated by them, but the expression on their faces was haughty. Sadly, one of them went blind as the years passed, but they both lived to be a goodly age.

It was a lovely, clean-looking modern red brick building, the post office, built in 1927, unlike the old one that had stood at the top of the hill just above the new building. The old one had been timber-framed and thatched and was demolished in 1939. John Snoxall was the sub-postmaster in 1910.

The post office that we knew is now a private house known as "Pound Cottage." It first moved from here to Mr. and Mrs. White's shop that once was Drage's, then became part of the present shopping centre in Lincoln Way, built in the 1960s.

When we had bought our sweets, we turned right into the main road again. To the left was a long, wide path that led to the "Rookery," made up of cottages, five of which were built by Revd George Ambrose Butler, vicar of Harlington, 1867-1870. Some of them were demolished in 1974. The rest have been demolished since. The Old Chapel yard, standing back from the main Sundon Road opposite the post office, also had cottages that are still lived in today. And then Joan and I reached the top of the hill, where the second pub of our journey stood,

"The Carpenters Arms". When Peter from Windsor was with us on his holidays, he was very fascinated by the horse mounting stone outside it. Peter lived in a public house in Windsor called "The Duke of Edinburgh," but it didn't have anything as wonderful as a horse mounting stone, he told us, and his imagination knew no bounds as he would tell us stories of his own making about stage coaches outside the old pub and all and sundry dismounting and remounting after they had had their fill of refreshments at "The Carpenters Arms." He wouldn't have been wrong in his imaginings, either. By the pub is a row of small cottages. In one of them when I was young lived Fanny Gazely who sold sweets from that cottage. Fanny once sat next to me during a service in the New Chapel. I wasn't very old. She always had a bag of sweets from her shop with her and she offered me one. 'Ooh!' I thought. 'Lovely'. But was it! After sucking for a few moments I thought I was being poisoned. Goodness knows what they were. Eucalyptus? Something much worse, my child's mind said to me. I wanted badly to spit it out and pop it under the chapel seat, but my older sister was watching me. So I had to swallow the hateful lump. After that occasion I squirmed in my pew if I saw Miss Fanny Gazely approaching and hoped she didn't sit next to me. Incidentally, she was not the Miss Gazely who played the "horgin" at the Sunday School, although I believe she was some relation.

On our walk we didn't need to stop at the shop on the Square very often as we had made our purchases where the two kind ladies smiled so sweetly at us. Mr. Jimmy Cleaver's was old with a stone floor and thick wooden counter but as we weren't very tall we couldn't see over top for the things we wanted.

Next to Jimmy Cleaver's shop, and right on the corner facing the War Memorial, there was a tiny cottage where a dear old quaint little lady lived. Her name was Ethel. Everyone knew her and liked her and was used to see her popping her head out of her door from time to time to see who was passing or who was waiting for the bus, because that was where it stopped. I was away from Harlington during the war when a Sherman Army tank on manoeuvres took a sharp turn on the bend where Ethel's cottage stood and caused it some damage. I can only wonder where Ethel was at the time, because apparently no-one was hurt! That cottage has since disappeared from the scene.

Carpenters Arms

This part of Harlington called "The Square" when I was young, calls forth thoughts of an appetising nature. Bays' fish and chip van arrived each week and there was a smell of "fish'n'chips" wafting through the village, making all and sundry feel really hungry. The van was a very large white vehicle with a hatch and counter let into the side through which Mr. Bays himself looked to serve his customers. He had a large, round, jolly face and on his head he wore a tall white Chef's hat, and although I was too short in those days to see the rest of him I knew he wore a white Chef's apron as the rest of his covering. The villagers would gather round the van and while waiting to be served would chatter away to each other, catching up on village and family news. Fish and chips were carried home in newspaper wrapping then, (first wrapped in greaseproof paper), long since discontinued of course as unhygienic and a health hazard and rightly so, but I never heard of anyone suffering because of it.

Another "happening" by the Square was the arrival of the fair in Bury Orchard, but I only remember its visit once when I was very young, although other villages have had fairs since. The fair was and is now called "The Statti", a name that derives from "Statute Fair," and it arrived round about October. Its main objective then was so that farmers and farm workers could meet there and discuss employment by those farmers for the workers on their land. This objective, of course, has long since gone by the board, no longer necessary with today's methods. There is still a visit from a fair once a year in autumn nowadays to Shefford, although not in the same style.

Fairs in the villages arrived with beautiful living caravans very immaculately bedecked with lace curtains and brasses flourishing at their windows, making a colourful scene with huge shining steam engines pulling the entourage. "Spit Rock" was made at one of the stalls, plaiting it by throwing it over a hook and stretching it and all the time spitting on the hands of the person making it - to stop it from sticking to them. Hence its name. And despite this, it sold like hot cakes!

But moving on towards Granny's... I suppose it was only natural at that age that we didn't take much notice of the War

Memorial on the Square, but in future years it came to mean a lot to me, remembering the deep devotion of our men to their country in the First and Second World Wars. Dedicated on May 9th 1920, it was re-dedicated in 1957, when a plaque was added for those who served in the 1939-45 war.

Now Joan and I were at the crossroads, one road leading to the station, one to Westoning, the one we had just walked up to Sundon and the fourth one we were about to take to the church. But first there was another shop that sold sweets, groceries and other things. Mr. and Mrs. Drage lived there with their son, Ken, who was the same age as my sister and her friends, all older than I was. Ken was very shy, but he had the advantage over other boys with his parents' sweet shop to help him tell a girl he adored her... In the shop there were some pretty coloured sweets with love messages on them - "Kiss Me," "Be Mine," (a bit forward that one for a boy so young in those days!) And of course, the ever longed for "I Love You." Perhaps a good name for those sweets would have been "Drage's Little Love Lumps!" The girls adored Ken and to receive his sweets was honour indeed and made their day.

All through the war years the shop once owned by the Drages was a village shop, with different owners coming and going after the Drage family left until one day it became a private house known as "The White House." Mr. and Mrs. White owned the shop at one point but it was not named after them. It simply became a white house when renovated, painted and decorated. As such it remains today.

Next to "The White House" we came to the School House where our headmistress lived, mentioned in chapter three about our school days, and the building opposite was then our school, now the Parish Hall.

We were now approaching the Church of St. Mary the Virgin, standing sentinel against the sky and dominating the village scene. Here, before we turned left for Granny's cottage, we had to pass my Great-uncle Charlie's abode. Before his retirement Great-uncle Charlie was manager of J.&W. Jones of Carner Hill Lime Works at Harlington, where a steam traction engine with the fascinating name of "Tasker's Little Giant" was used until 1947 for scraping the chalk from the face of the quarry and for transporting the lime to Harlington station.

Parish Hall

When I became a journalist in my adult years, I became good friends with Great-uncle Charlie's youngest son, Don. He also had wished to go into journalism but was unable to do so because of a physical disablement. Neither was he able to join the forces in the Second World War for the same reason. So, as there was land by his father's cottage, Don had a very nice grocery shop there and it was well used by the villagers. Don married a Scottish girl who was a great help to him in his business.

Tasker s Steam Engine

Don s Shop

Great-uncle Charlie and his family lived in one of two adjoining cottages, listed collectively as Straw Plaiters House. In the cottage the other side, potatoes and other things were sold. The straw plait trade had been very prominent in years past in Harlington. Plaiting schools became well established at the beginning of the 19th century and in Harlington a Mrs. Chandler ran the one most well known. It was Mrs. Chandler who was responsible for a wage scale for plaiters being presented to the Poor Law Commissioners. "The Harlington Arms" public house was a collecting point for straw plait work because it was in Station Road. One time residents at Harlington Manor House, the Lye family owned a factory in Luton for dyeing and bleaching straw plait. The decline of straw plaiting came when children had to attend compulsory schooling and were no longer able to do the work full time. I'm glad I was not a straw plait child. I was very happy at school and would not have liked to miss out on it.

Round the corner from Great-uncle Charlie's was and still is a late 19th century residence standing well back from the road. In it lived a little girl named Betty Morris who was a friend of mine before she moved away from Harlington. Members of the Morris family must have lived there for years, because at one time a Mr. Morris, resident, was the manager of Forder's Brickworks at Westoning.

Opposite the old cemetery, so peaceful in the shadow of the church, little cottages still nestle as they lead up to "Mulberry Cottage," Granny Harris' old home. One of them, number 27, has signs that once an elementary school was held there. A number of used slate pencils have been found outside the front window and also a small amount of worked plait was discovered in the attic. This could be the one called the "Straw Bonnet". Fascinating name. And then suddenly, there it was and will, I hope, remain, the old white picturesque homestead, standing a long way back from the road. Joan and I must have been ready to sit down for a few minutes before starting back to our part of the village, and to receive whatever Granny Harris would replenish us with.

Straw Plaiters House

"Mulberry Cottage" has a tranquil ancient setting, with the 14th century church of St. Mary the Virgin towering majestically on the opposite side of the road, and cannot fail to catch the eye of visitors as they pass through Harlington, perhaps on their way to Barton-le-Clay. The cottage stands out white and resplendent. It is timber framed, of the 17th century, and there, by the garage, can be seen a Mulberry tree that must be mighty old, too! The Mulberry tree was introduced into England and France so that Silkworm larvae can feed on the leaves, the Silkworm Moth having been distributed from China throughout the world. At Harlington School there was silkworm larvae which needed to be fed, so Mulberry leaves were given by the owners of the cottage, although the larva does feed also on lettuce and the foliage of the Osage orange. The Silkworm Moth itself does not eat and seldom flies and it only has a brief adult life of about three days when the female lays between three hundred to five hundred eggs. Watching for the process of pupation which occurs within the cocoon made of white or yellow silken thread was an intriguing study for school, although the silkworms did not appear to be present when I was there, but they were in my sister's school days.

Granny Harris died in 1943 and, on the death of Joan's Uncle Slimmy, Mulberry Cottage was sold as a beautiful oldeworlde residence and as such it remains today. But many old Harlingtonians will remember when it was at one time divided into two homes, as at Straw Plaiters House, where Great uncle Charlie lived. Then, two members of the Ashby family lived, one at each end, Miss Nancy Ashby and Mrs. Jessie Delve. They were both Harlington school caretakers at different times.

Walking to Granny's was fun and for two youngsters, a happy adventure to be remembered through the years.

Mulberry Cottage

Chapter Eight

Old Homesteads Remembered

Joan's Granny was not the only relative I shared with her. On moving from my Bute Cottage home to live next door to her in Sundon Road, I enjoyed going with her to visit her Auntie Liz and Uncle Bill Avery. Uncle Bill worked for the railway, so he and Auntie Liz lived in one of the railway cottages, as my own aunt and uncle, Mabel and Horace Asbury, had done before they bought and lived in my old Bute Cottage home. The terraced 1870s red brick built cottages for employees of the Midland Railway Company are now privately owned and enlarged. The back gardens that belonged to the tenants in the old days are smaller because part of them became the development of Park Leys, stretching round into the fields where I used to ramble and where I used to live in Sundon Road. Adjoining the last cottage was the Weighbridge office to the coal and goods yard with Franklin's Coals office opposite. The Weighbridge office has since been demolished and a new office stands where the Franklin's Coals office once was, now used for other things.

The folk who lived in Station Road didn't have far to go for their beer, for only a few steps up the road in the direction of the Square was "The Harlington Arms" public house. Built in 1871, the pub was extended in 1901 and had stables for two carts, a trap, a pony and two horses. A cart was used to load items to take to the station because the public house made a good distribution point, particularly for those ladies who did straw hat work at home before it went to Luton hat businesses.

A photograph shows the publican, Mr. Albert Bonner and Mrs. Bonner who has a little dog in her arms. It may have been a pekinese. But I understand from a relative of hers she also had a large, black dog at some time and my sister remembers it sitting outside the public house, watching the world go by.

No 7. Station Road

"The Harlington Arms" became a private residence in 1960 and the stables were converted into a pottery in 1980, though it is now closed. The former public house is very welcoming; I have seen where the old snug bar was and it is now the main entrance hall, wide and spacious. The establishment is now known as No.7 Station Road. The main door from outside contains over the top of it some very neat, hidden electrical lighting let into what was part of the original large window. From the entrance hall, steps down lead into what was once the public bar. It has made a superb, comfortable lounge. At the back of this home is a long pine table with matching chairs in the kitchen, which has an inspired feature - on the main wall a unique picture, painted on the tiles, of a very famous beautiful local scene, the Sharpenhoe Clappers. The householder at the time of writing has made the fine table of pine himself and is the artist of the picture. He is also responsible for numerous models, amongst them an intricately made model of a watermill and house with furniture and fittings to scale.

Almost behind the public house were two cottages now made into one. At one time nurse Jessie Butcher lived in one of them and in the other, Cllr. Bill Brown. Jessie was a district nurse who brought many babies into the world in the district. Buxom with a no-nonsense air about her and very efficient, she was highly respected. I remember seeing her walking her dog, a West Highland Terrier named Jock, through the village. On her retirement she moved into sheltered accommodation in Ampthill, this in the days before Harlington's own flats with warden in Orchard House. She died in Ampthill on 29th May 1999 aged 96 years.

Opposite what was once "The Harlington Arms" is a half-timbered framed 16th century Manor Farm house, one of the oldest buildings in the village. But there the old scene ends, for new houses have been built in the grounds of the farm house, and now form Wentworth Court. Most of the new roads and closes take their names from some part of Harlington's history and Wentworth Court is no exception. A loss to the community are the timber framed 18th century thatched barns of Manor Farm which were demolished in 1989! But at least the cowsheds remain, or some of them. I remember in my youth coming off the train on my way home with other folk. Passing those cow sheds by Manor Farm we had to step warily to avoid the cow pats dropped by the cows being brought in for milking. And we didn't always miss them!

I am left wondering why Station Road was once called Ampthill Street. It seems a long way round to Ampthill from that part of Harlington, but perhaps the Westoning roadway, the obvious way to Ampthill from my young days onward, was still a track and the cottages in which we lived were not built.

At the bottom of Station Road, turning to the right away from the station, the very long road leads to a lake well stocked with coarse fish - it is claimed that a carp thirty years old survives there, so it's not surprising that fishermen have been buying tickets for years now, parking their cars and spending a few hours in the peaceful surroundings. But the setting has improved considerably since my young days, for then it was known as "The Brickyard" and the little cottages that accompanied it were called "Brickyard Cottages." In one of them before I was born lived the large, jolly lady of our picnic years. Before marriage she was Miss Mabel Hinks, then she became Mrs, Pearson, and later, on the death of her first husband, she became Mrs. Croxford and as such I knew her when she lived with her family in one of the Sunnymede Villas in Sundon Road. When I attended Harlington village school Mrs. Croxford helped make the summer holidays of our picnic-on-the-hills group, of which her own son, Dennis, was one, even more carefree and enjoyable. There was never a dull moment when she was present. She can be seen centre position in the photograph of the "Old Brickyard Cottages", and judging by that photo she hadn't changed much from that time to when I first knew her when I was the age of nine or ten.

The "Old Brickyard Cottages" have certainly been transformed since those days. They are now a complete dwelling with the inspired name of "Briarwood", enhanced by its lake and exclusive estate. Until recently it was owned by Mr. and Mrs. Rix and it has been a unique venue for official Harlington Parish Church events with Sheila Rix working commendably hard as hostess. Sheila moved after her husband died in 1998.

Brickyard Cottages

It may be wondered why this part of Harlington was once called a brickyard. In The Survey of Bedfordshire Brickmaking by Alan Cox Nov 1979 we are given the facts. Alan Cox states it was shown as a brickfield on a map surveyed 1881-82 but it probably ceased operation shortly after 1885, as it was not shown on a map published in 1901.

Travelling up into the village from "Briarwood" to Barton Road, almost at the other end of Harlington are Pretoria Cottages. In one of them lived my other childhood friend, Brenda. When I wasn't with Joan I was always with her. She lived in the second one of the cottages with her parents, Mr. and Mrs. Alfred Saunders. Her older sister, Gwen, had left to be a Children's Nurse, but when she came home on her days off she often took Brenda and me out somewhere for a treat. I'm afraid Brenda and I were two little mischiefs when we got together and played Gwen up somewhat, which was rather different from when I was with Joan, who was a quiet little girl! Gwen died in February, 2001, aged 83 years, in Leighton Buzzard.

In the first of Pretoria Cottages right by the Barton Road cemetery resided my mother's uncle, Sid Brinklow and his wife, Auntie Min. Uncle Sid was Brenda's godfather and yet another of Grandma Lucy's brothers (the Brinklows were a large family and today Harlington has a good representation of my third cousins!)

Pretoria Cottages are named after the Boer War and are divided into three sections by plaques on their front walls: numbers 1-15 inscribed "Pretoria Cottages 1900"; numbers 17-23 a plaque inscribed "J & W.G. 1901"; and numbers 25-31 a plaque "J. & W. Giles 1901." They were built of yellow brick with Welsh slate roofs for £100 each for farm workers and their families. Since the days when I used to visit Brenda they have been considerably improved and, although they were pleasant enough homes before, they are now extremely comfortable.

A favourite childhood place of mine was "Rose Cottage", just up the road from my own home in Sundon Road. I was always welcomed there with great warmth and affection by Great-aunt May and Uncle Jack. As I ran up the steps and into their home I would usually find them sitting one each side of the old fireplace. An olde-worlde cottage of considerable charm and interest, the small garden at the front had rose trees sweeping down to the road, so it was aptly named. Like Great - aunt May and Uncle Jack the rose trees are now gone and this 17th century timber framed cottage presents a different image today.

This old pair would love to tell me about the outbuilding across the yard from the cottage. It was once a slaughter house in the days when meat was sold from there, but I didn't care for that story, imagining the blood and the animals in my young mind. However, by the time I had reached home I was ready for a meal and had forgotten about the gory details that slaughter house had conjured up and I was eager for the meal placed before me, even if it was meat!

Asphodel Cottage

There were many wonders of their home that Great-aunt May and Uncle Jack knew little about and I had to wait a goodly number of years to learn about them myself. I wonder what they would say if they knew their old home, "Rose Cottage" is now known as "Asphodel", a name that carries with it a rather intriguing story... A young woman and her test pilot husband moved into Great-aunt May's cottage after she and Uncle Jack had died. They bought it and because they had a Saluki dog with the Kennel name of "Asphodel," they renamed their cottage after it. I met this young lady just after I was married and had a very interesting conversation with her. She was looking distressed and searching outside her gate for the Saluki's puppies that had squeezed through into the road. I helped her find them and we became friendly. She told me she taught ballet. Mr. and

Mrs. Richard Dudley bought the cottage in 1965. They acquired a kind of lily that grows amongst the rocks in Greece, because it is called the "Asphodel Lily". It now flourishes in the garden of their cottage. During a visit in 1999 they showed me round and I was greatly impressed by the change of scene since my relatives' days. The cottage is so restful that I was loathe to leave. Richard told me about the inglenook fireplace in the first room that was revealed during restoration work. Once, he said, it must have had an open hearth and a chimney structure of a kind similar to the early Smoke Hood type. One of the rooms of "Asphodel" appears to have been a dairy with sunken floor at one time. In the Victorian era and in modern times other rooms were added, I learned.

In the cottage I was shown a very small boot with laces, one of a pair that were found bricked up in an alcove beside the fireplace and dated, it would seem, at about 1760 according to the method of eyelet manufactured then. This practice, the concealing of old boots or shoes, was a superstition to ward off evil spirits. Pat and Richard drew my attention to the "Smoke Hole" at the side of the fireplace where sides of bacon were smoked in the old days and then they pointed out to me the ancient meat hooks that were still hanging from the centre beam. By the side of the "Smoke Hole" is the bread oven. Mm! I could almost smell the bread baking!

I was also shown a very old piece of lace that had been worked many years before. It looked as though it might have been a pattern for lacemaking, perhaps in the days when that trade with the straw plait was prevalent in Harlington. As we made our way into the garden, the dog, a dear old spaniel, lumbered after us and looked up at me with liquid eyes, pleading to be fussed. I thought back for a moment to the Saluki that had once lived there. This was indeed a home that any animal could surely be happy in, content with its lot! And there in the garden was an old apple tree and accompanying it a very ancient, rustic well to add to the scene of olde-worlde charm.

Great-aunt May knew nothing of the wonders of her dear old homestead. If she had, she would have said in her typical country style, 'Well, I'm blowed!'

Sunny days and funny days,
Sometimes not much money days;
Zippy days and nippy days,
Lovely Serendippy days.
Oh, those complex childhood ways,
Those days of long ago!

Wistful times and dreamy times,
Sunday school and Church bell chimes;
Childhood walks and secret talks,
Ginger beer and popping corks.
Do we need the knives and forks
For picnics on the hills?'

Memories will always stay
Of that lovely yesterday.
Childhood cheeks were all aglow
In that magic long ago.
Would that it could still be so,
But years just roll away!

(Edna L. Wilsher.)

Chapter Nine

"Your Country Needs You"

The message came through loud and clear when war commenced on Sunday 3rd. September 1939. I've often thought 'What a day to start a war!' The most holy day of the week as it was then, although obviously not observed as such by many now.

The message was on one of numerous posters displayed throughout the country to encourage the citizens of Britain to do their best and help the country win the War against Germany. And Harlington responded in full. Another poster told us to "Dig For Victory." Harlington married women, usually the older ones not on factory work or in the Forces because of family commitments, rallied to the call and worked on the land, helping the farmers. Some of them had done land work for a number of years before, so they just continued their pea picking (the peasers they were called), brussels sprouting, potato harvesting and gleaning, a lorry picking them up each day and taking them to their destination. In my early school days I remember it was Wood Farm along the Sundon Road where I lived, the road that led one way to the hills and the other to the village of Sundon. They were a happy, laughing crowd. The land girls also worked at Wood Farm. My friend Brenda joined the Land Army in later years after first serving in the A.T.S. As the war progressed, though, farmers took on Italian prisoners-of-war for land work.

Hat factory workers, of whom there were many in Harlington, were soon called up for war work in the Luton munition factories because hat work was listed as being a luxury trade. My sister was older than myself and therefore called for war service before I was. She worked in the war years at Vauxhall Motors where heavy Bedford vehicles and Churchill tanks were made. She was called up from her work in the Packing section of a Luton hat factory, after the war returning to the hat trade in the Buying section. It must have been a great relief for all concerned that the big daylight bombing raid, when Vauxhall Motors was hit, happened when my sister and her fellow workers from Harlington were not there.

A factory on the site of an old brickyard was known as Harlington Production Tools during the war and employed a large number of Harlington people and those from surrounding villages. It had been evacuated from London (Islington) to Harlington for safety from the bombing there. The employees were picked up by old Army lorries from a point in Barton to do war work in the factory. It was situated just on the corner on the opposite side of the Sharpenhoe Road where both the old Harlington Mill stands (long since disused), and what was then Burgoyne's Market Garden, now Mill End Nurseries. Fresh vegetables for the factory canteen were delivered by Mr. Keith Burgoyne and deposited for coolness in one of the old brick kilns of the factory. Many happy times were spent by the workers and their friends at dances held there and many a couple must have had a romantic moonlight saunter back to Harlington! After the war the factory was taken over first by British Oxygen, then by Carboloy and last by Sandvik, thus becoming known as Carboloy/Sandvik in later years. The site is privately owned at this time of writing.

Harlington had its Local Defence Volunteers, later known as the Home Guard, to defend the country on home ground against invasion and they were successful in capturing two Germans in the area surrounding the village, one having bailed out from his German aircraft. (The Home Guard was disbanded eventually in December 1945).

The A.R.P. (Air Raid Precautions) had their wardens, of whom my father was one. Among his duties was the distribution of gas masks. Toddlers had gas masks resembling Mickey Mouse and other Disneyland characters, while for babies there were special respirators in which they could lie and have air pumped through to them. Not a chink of light had to show through the windows of houses, so there was a rush to get blackout curtains fitted. My father and his fellow members of the A.R.P. patrolled the village nightly to ensure that everywhere was in absolute darkness and, if not, the words rang out loudly, 'Put that light out!' A.R.P. headquarters were at the Manor, a central position by the Square. Mrs. Pamela Daniels, elder daughter of Major and Mrs. Tabor was in charge and they were also used as a First Aid post, first aid tuition being given in the village.

Harlington Manor

Bombs fell in the village and along its outposts, but I was not actually living at home at the time, as I was by then on war service. I heard of the incidents from my family. I was told of a Vl flying bomb that fell near the Bunyan's Oak tree out of the village, but causing some confusion and damage. Another occurred when I was on weekend leave from the A.T.S., having crept home in the early hours by the first train in the morning to stop at Harlington Station, so that I might get a bit of rest from the buzz bombs that were falling thick and fast in London.The bomb fell in a field near Wood Farm. Fortunately no-one was hurt. My mother told us to "Get under the table, quick!" I don't know what good she thought that would do. I had come so close many times during each day to being blown apart in London and we just looked upon it as part of the day's routine. But I never told my mother as I didn't wish to worry her. There was another bomb that fell by Dyers Hall where the elderly people had been evacuated, but I think they had been moved elsewhere for safety again by then, and of course the Army were using it for firing practice.

Not least of Harlington's war experiences was the arrival of the evacuees from London. This story is told last of all because their arrival surely had a considerable impact on Harlington's image, an image that began to change from then on. Through the following years many more people from London and other places descended on our little old sleepy village (although we didn't think it was sleepy!), and a hive of activity was brought about mainly through the newcomers. These people had new ideas and set the pace for Harlington's entry into this fast changing age. But the evacuees themselves from London, it seemed, were the forerunners with their different lifestyle and Harlington must have appeared at first to have been rather slow to them.

I had been away from the village school a few years. studying to be a journalist, when the evacuation of school children from London began on Friday 1st September 1939. They arrived in Luton where a main receiving centre awaited them and from there they were sent on to various dispersal units and distributed between Luton and the surrounding areas. Walthamstow schools were the first to arrive. Harlington received pupils from the William Morris Selective Central Boys' School with a number of girls and some smaller children for good measure. The two dear little girls who were billeted on Miss Slade mentioned in "Walking to Granny's" were amongst them. They arrived with their big brother, one of the Walthamstow School pupils, but he was billeted at another house.

It must have been a heartrending experience for the very young evacuees leaving their homes and especially saying goodbye to their mothers and travelling to a strange place, even though it was only just up the line from London. They must have wondered when they would see their parents again. However, some of the mothers visited quite often. It must have made it difficult, though, for the host family to make the food rations stretch when this happened, although I'm sure everyone was made welcome in Harlington. The original Govt. Billeting payments recorded in that wonderfully informative book, "Luton At War" compiled by the Luton News, 1947 of Home Counties Newspapers Ltd. Group where I began my journalistic career, is: children 10-14 years, 10s. 6d; 14-16 years, 12s. 6d; and 16 years and over, 15s. If more than one child was billeted on a house, the host family received 8s.6d. per child. It was reviewed later on.

Most of the evacuees were of the age range fourteen to sixteen years in Harlington, with about three of them coming up to seventeen years. Those three were Paul and Peter (yes, really!), billeted at Wood Farm and tall, lanky Sid, known as "Skid" because he rode a motor bike round the village in a mad fashion. Skid, it would seem, took a shine to me and would look at me in an intensely endearing way when we chanced to meet and I would blush profusely and try to hide behind the person or persons I was with. But Skid took off to goodness knows where when he came of age to leave Walthamstow school and I thought I would see him no more. Lo and behold, however, years after the war when I had returned from my war service in the A.T.S and was back at the Luton News office, then at the corner of Alma Street, Luton (its frontage was in Manchester Street), lanky Skid suddenly appeared from the confines of the Alma Street cinema, now Luton County Court, although he didn't appear to have his motor bike with him anywhere, unless he had it hidden away somewhere round the back of the building! Both Peter and Paul, I was told, left for Colchester College to further their education when they had finished at Walthamstow School.

Aunt Patti (who laid the Foundation stone of The New Methodist Chapel), it seemed, was not too old to have two boys of about fifteen to sixteen billeted on her and I'm sure they would have been very well looked after with Aunt Patti's large family around to help. They were quiet boys. One had a very quaint name. I think it might have been a nickname, it was so strange. It was "Mepha!" Mr. Steve Smith, our dairyman, had an evacuee named Malcolm, again a very quiet lad who always looked perplexed.

A very nice sixteen years old was Ken who went to the Methodist Church every Sunday and was highly thought of there. His billet home was with Mr. and Mrs. Chappell who lived right at the top of the Sundon Road hill before turning into the Square. They must have gleaned great comfort from having him, for their own son, Reg., was serving in the Army and eventually became a prisoner-of-war in Japan. Reg. did return home again after the war and married a very dear friend of mine, Doris, known as Topper to her closest friends. But that's another story to be told later.

We were fortunate in Harlington to have such well behaved and nicely spoken evacuees. Not so a friend of ours living in a neighbouring village... Two young lads descended upon her and her husband, a farm worker. Because of his work he received an extra large food allowance of cheese. It was therefore quite natural for his wife to feed her little Londoners a quantity of cheese dishes. One day one of the lads looked at his supper plate, pulled a wry face and said, 'Watcha fink we are, Missis? Bleedin' mice?'. The lady replied in no uncertain terms, 'You use that language to me again m'lad and I'll run you all the way back to London. Now, stop your cheek and get on with your supper or I'll send you to bed without it.' Another time this lady opened her door to the two lads returning from school to be met with, 'Missis P., Patsy's pooped 'is trarsis '(trousers.) What she said should not be printed. Patsy must have been short for "Patrick."

Harlington village school children shared their studies with the evacuees. Miss Colman having left the scene as Harlington's headmistress, Mrs. Slade took over. A second Harlington teacher was Miss Powley.

Three masters came down with the Walthamstow school, Mr. Hall (B.Sc) with his wife and baby; Mr. G.R. (Gus) Easton (B.A.), who was the headmaster until he was called up in 1941 when Mr. Hall took over. He also had his wife and child with him. The third teacher changed as time went on. All the school children, Walthamstow and Harlington, were sectioned off into two buildings, the village school and the Old Chapel rooms, where we used to hold our Sunday School.

The third teacher that I remember was the one who eventually became billeted on us. Mr. Brown the billeting officer asked us to take him when he moved from another billet. As we had no evacuees, but one spare bedroom, my parents agreed. So Thomas Carson entered our lives and we had many pleasurable hours in his company. He was an Australian, a kindly man of about forty years, very quietly spoken, with calm features that made you feel at ease. He could, however, rise to the occasion when roused, as became evident through an incident at the school...

A certain village boy one day tried his patience to the limit. The lad lived near us. His granny looked after him while his mother was out at work and even his granny often found him unmanageable. One afternoon my mother went into the little scullery just off from the kitchen to find her small curtain rod of bamboo had been taken out of the top of the curtains and they were lying neatly folded on the draining board. Of course, she was mystified, but during the afternoon the boy's granny popped her head round the door after furiously knocking. She was most aggressive. 'Where's that b----- schoolmaster?' she demanded. Every word was a swear word from granny. Mother was startled, but light dawned on her darkness as granny continued, 'My grandchild has been caned by that man from down under. You tell him to go back there or I'll ... (The mind boggles at what she would do to him.) My mother's reply didn't help matters, 'Well, granny,' she said, 'all I can say is that grandson of yours must have deserved it. The man from down under wouldn't have caned him if he hadn't. He's too kind for that.' The air was blue with strong language for a few short moments, then granny slammed the door so hard that it almost shook the house down and she was gone. When Mr. Carson arrived back at tea-time, mother held her curtains up. 'Look,' she said. 'Where is it, then?' meaning the curtain rod. Mr. Carson produced it from behind his back and smiled awkwardly. Then he said in his quiet voice, 'Sorry!', and proceeded to tell her what a horror the lad had been that morning and how he had taken the rod from her curtains when he came home at lunch time, thinking what a superb cane it would make. My parents laughed often through the years at the memory of this episode.

I was very sad when Thomas Carson left to join the Australian Army and I went to the station with him to wave goodbye. As the train drew out of the station he gave me a wonderful smile, lifted his hand in farewell and said, 'Take care, little Edna. See you again some day.' But I never did. Thomas Carson had gone out of our lives for ever.

Mr. Carson's parting gift to me was the address of a young Australian girl student he used to teach. She became my penfriend for many years - through my journalistic days, through my time in the A.T.S. and for some time into my married life. She became a nursing sister in Parkes District Hospital, Australia and after marrying at a much later age than myself, she went to live in the Bush, where she had two children, with her husband who was a wealthy businessman. I never met her. I regret that I didn't visit Australia and that she didn't come over to England to see me after the war. I'm sure she would have been extremely interested to see the olde-worlde cottage I was living in when I married. It was after my marriage that I received a letter from her mother in Australia, then a very old lady, telling me of her daughter's death at the age of forty years.

As time passed in the war years, some of the evacuees from Walthamstow left, but those still in the village shared with us some happy events. The concert in the Old Chapel, for instance, at which Mrs. Easton, the headmaster's wife in her trained, beautiful mezzo soprano voice gave us a rendering of "The Holy City" - which left a lasting impression upon us. This is not the only thing that Mrs. Easton will be remembered for in the village, for she was the initiator of a Primary Sunday School at Harlington Methodist Church and also their first Primary Leader. After her return to London, my sister took over.

Other items on the programme at the Old Chapel were some mandolin solos by my mother and me, one of which was helped along by a guest artiste from a neighbouring town with her harpsicord. This was "In An Eighteenth Century Drawing-room." Other than that we were accompanied by the Methodist Church organist at the piano, Miss Kitty Chambers. A very tall girl who had come to Harlington with the Walthamstow School as an evacuee also took part in the concert. She was a talented tap dancer and singer of popular songs.

The artistes were introduced by our very pretty beauty queen, chosen at the "Wings For Victory" celebrations in May, 1943, when money was raised to help buy more Spitfires and suchlike. By kind permission of Major and Mrs. Tabor, Harlington Manor grounds were the venue for a garden fete, and the setting lent itself admirably for the occasion.

During all this time I had been studying for my entry into journalism and one day my career took off. I became a cub reporter on the staff of Home Counties Newspapers, Ltd., Luton, the firm owned by Messrs. Richard and John Gibbs.

Chapter Ten

"Thursday Is News Day."

I had seen the words prominently displayed in yellow on black on the railway bridge that led into Luton town centre many times when I had visited the town with my mother and friends. But this time it was different. THIS time it was a very pointed reminder that I was on my way AT THAT VERY MOMENT to the actual place where the news was being published for Luton and the surrounding district which included Harlington. A few minutes before I had stepped from the train that had brought me into Luton from Harlington with flutterings in my heart and stomach at the thought of what lay before me, the adventure into the realm of journalism that I had looked forward to for so long. At last it had ARRIVED. My career was about to take off.

Luton News offices, with clock

I entered the building through the front office in Manchester Street and was shown up the wide, impressive looking stairway to the top floor, along a corridor, passing the room of the Woman's Editor and thence coming to the "sanctum" where the Great I Am of Sport dwelt - Mr. Jack Hunt, Sports Editor, known as "Crusader", the name under which he wrote and by which he will be remembered by many older people. And then I came to the "Graveyard!". Somewhat daunting? Not really. It was only the filing room before the advances of today's methods took over. Records were kept there of people who had hit the headlines one way or another and even the deaths etcetera of the Man In the Street, these reports all being written up in the three Luton papers, "The Luton News," "Tuesday Pictorial" and "Saturday Telegraph." The "Green 'Un" was the sports paper in which "Crusader" held sway and this was also published on Saturdays and had a considerable following not only in the town but also in the little surrounding villages. The newspapers were delivered in my village by van to the post office, where Mrs. Mabel Hill dealt with them for distribution. It was a yellow van, eagerly awaited by the villagers. On its side was written in black lettering the words "HOME COUNTIES NEWSPAPERS LTD," but never during the war years was the place name "Luton" displayed. THAT would have been giving secrets away to the enemy! As I worked at "The Luton News" I had a free paper to take home every week.

That very first day as a junior reporter brings back some humorous memories- the heavy door, for example, that swung back before I had the chance to make my escape; the sea of faces that turned and stared at me as I timidly entered that domain of male reporters, young and not so young. A GIRL? Yes, a girl had dared to enter their world. Still, they looked at me with interest, so I gave them my brightest smile, although trembling within. A middle-aged man greeted me. The chief reporter, known affectionately, I learned, as "Buckie," short for Mr. Buckman. He showed me the desk that I was to look upon as mine if I was lucky! I had to qualify for it first, though, I knew. I had to show them the stuff I was made of and in the days that followed I had to tolerate a good bit of teasing- tweakings of my hair and a pinch or two on my arms and, if I hadn't sat well and truly firm upon it, no doubt my bottom would have received the same treatment, most certainly looked upon as taboo these days! And when I looked at the centre disc on the telephone at my desk - the old-fashioned kind, of course- I found it had a message specifically for any girl reporters who might sit there. It read, "Be clever, sweet maid, and let who will be good." I noticed after that that each phone on the other desks sported a message for its occupant. My desk was obviously chosen for me because of that special phone message! Well, I suppose it added to the spice of life in the reporters' room. Buckie was a kind man, but even so he looked hard at me that first day as he told me that journalism has rules that must be obeyed. One of them was, "When in doubt, find out or leave out," a rule I still adhere to in my present day writings.

Luton News , Front Office

On a shelf over the old-fashioned fireplace stood a large diary in which was entered all the jobs that were to be undertaken each day and the initials of the respective reporters who were to undertake them. I found myself reporting funerals and writing up weddings from a form sent in by the bridal couple, some of whom lived in Harlington and often thought I could work the oracle and give them extra space for their write-up (how could I explain to them that at that stage in my life I was a mere nobody on the editorial staff and of not much consequence?); and then there was the task of ringing round the churches in Luton and district and taking details from their vicars of forthcoming events to be put on THE DIARY. I was the little cub reporter and as such I was certainly not allowed to have anything to do with the Luton Sack Murder that happened at about that time. "Too young," I was told. "Not a job for a girl, anyway," murmured the chief reporter. So I sighed and stuck to the minor jobs, with ambition, however, burning strongly in my breast.

And then one day it happened and I was no longer the little Miss Nobody of the reporting room... I was sent to report details of an Ecclesiastical assembly with the then Bishop of St. Albans, Dr. Michael Furze, as the honourable speaker. Once again the "collywobbles" started up in my stomach as he approached me. There I stood, a small slip of a girl wearing an Alice Band to keep my curls tidy, low heeled girlish shoes and trying not to look nervous. But I needn't have worried. It was as though he knew how I felt. 'Come,' he said, 'we'll have a cup of tea while I sort out a copy of my speech for you.' He was tall and gaunt, but his coal black eyes were kind and a gentle smile played about his thin features. That was the first time I was on duty as a journalist at such a gathering, but it was not the last. I met Dr. Michael Furze on numerous occasions after that and no more did those saucy male reporters tweak my hair and pinch my arms. I was treated with respect from then on. My father, too, devout church man at Harlington that he was, was impressed, although he told me in very serious tones to be sure and live up to those special tasks that came my way. My father remembered the time (28th July 1929) when Dr. Furze dedicated the very beautiful John Bunyan window designed by Warren Wilson for the Church of St. Mary the Virgin, Harlington. The then vicar of Harlington Parish Church was the Revd. Arthur George Hodgson who baptised me. Mr Hodgson's retirement from Harlington took place shortly after the memorable event of, the dedication of the window which portrays a scene from Bunyan's, "The Pilgrim's Progress" ("Do,you see yonder shining light?").

There were many nights when I was late home because of my work. Young journalists, even girls, had no concessions. But it didn't worry me. I was too engrossed in my journalistic life and I knew my parents would not worry overmuch if I was late home, because an arrangement had been made with Ray Walton at the garage just along the road from my parents' house that I would phone him and give him a message for them and he would see it was delivered. The part that I didn't really like was coming off the train at Harlington station if it was late and my father, who worked there, was not on duty. Then I had to make my own way home alone, as there were no street lights at that time in the village.

Apart from reporting events in and around Luton, I was expected to be present at happenings in Harlington because I lived there. Not least were the Parish Council meetings, especially if there was something of importance on the agenda. Sometimes this task clashed with my town work and I had to make my own arrangements to pick up details from someone else in the village. It was fortunate, then, that I had a very good friend in Esme Whiskin. She often obliged and I would collect details from her house which stood at the highest point in Harlington along the Barton road overlooking the lovely nearby hills. It was then, natural that she should have some of her ashes scattered on the Clappers when she died in October 1997. The rest were scattered in other places dear to her heart.

Esme kept a good account of Harlington happenings and she and her husband Peter gave loyally of their services to the village, Esme serving on the Parish Council and Peter on the District and County Councils. They worked particularly hard to help Harlington achieve its Village Hall. She was the granddaughter of the late George Lansbury, MP and was related to Angela Lansbury the actress. Esme's daughter, Katherine, also went into theatrical work and is known as Kate Lansbury. She has made a film on video for 20th Century Fox called "Ever After." Kate's son, Billie, is also an actor and her other son, Sean, is a singer and script writer. Kate remembers the Village Pageant of Harlington that took place during the opening of the Village Hall on the 9th September 1950, when at the age of ten years she took the part of a page, with two beagles on a lead.

Junior reporting days were very happy for me and I always wondered, as I set out in the morning from Harlington to catch the train at the little station for Luton, what the day would hold for me. But I was certainly surprised one day on arriving in the reporters' room to be informed by the chief reporter that I was to have an added task to do. I was to be "Uncle Geofree" of the Children's Page (and yes, Uncle Geofree WAS spelt that way. It had been by a former Children's Page writer and I had to follow suit so as not to confuse the young readers.) 'Look in the files,' said Buckie, 'and take it from there.' And that was all I had to go by, but it did not bother me because I had written children's stories since I was old enough to do so and the job was right up my street.

Chapter Eleven

Harlington House.

As I studied the Children's Page features that had been written in the previous Tuesday Pictorial editions, I felt that the stories for the children and the little letters from Uncle Geofree, although pleasing enough, somehow lacked that extra something to make them sparkle and for the children to want more. So I set about the task of accomplishing this, hoping it would meet with the approval of those in authority "below stairs" where the editorial staff lived! Having made sure when my next day off was to be, I put my plan in motion and rang Mrs. Tabor of Harlington Manor, or Harlington House as it is historically recorded. She was genuinely pleased to grant me an interview on my day off, although I'm sure she thought it was for a strange reason, that of hearing about her treasured antiques and of writing them up into stories, half fiction, half truth in Uncle Geofree's Children's Page in "The Tuesday Pictorial" each week. Mrs. Tabor had never had such a thing happen to her before and she greeted the idea with great enthusiasm. She told my mother when next she saw her, 'What an unusual little gel you have for a daughter, Mrs. Lane!' I can well imagine what my mother's reply was! 'Yes, a bit too unusual. I never know what she's going to do next!'

On the afternoon in question I set off up the road from our house well groomed and on my best behaviour for the timber framed Harlington Manor that stood by the Square. Its history is colourful, but as this is not a history book I will keep

85

information about the Manor down to a minimum, apart from my favourite subject of John Bunyan. Suffice it to say that the present Harlington Manor House was built circa 1500, the original Manor House having been built in the 13th-14th century in another part of Harlington known as Upper East End. Mrs. Tabor was eager to tell the story of John Bunyan and his strong connection with the Manor as she showed me around her gracious home, this after we had taken tea, served very daintily in a room looking out on to the Manor grounds where so many events took place through the years, and after she had extolled the beauties and backgrounds of her beloved antique treasures from which I was inspired to write stories for my young Children's Page readers.

As a staunch devotee of John Bunyan I listened with deep interest as she told me about him and of how he came to be connected with the Manor. Unfortunately, many people confuse the story of where he was arrested, believing it to be at the Manor House. Mrs. Tabor was aware of this and made certain that I knew the correct story, making it quite clear that his arrest took place at a meeting of the Independent Church at a farm-house at Samsell in the Westoning area.

The house is not now there, but the site, still identified, is a very significant part of Bunyan history. John Bunyan was taken from Samsell to Harlington Manor House where he was interrogated after a delay caused by the absence of Francis Wingate, magistrate (Harlington Manor was held by the Wingate family for a very long time. Henrietta Maria who became the queen of King Charles I was at one time tutored by Edmond Wingate.) The interrogation was undertaken by Francis Wingate, Revd William Lindell, the then vicar of Harlington and by a Bedford lawyer, William Foster. Refusing to agree not to preach to unauthorised religious gatherings, Bunyan stood trial at Bedford and was in the County Gaol there for twelve years, where that wonderful book, "The Pilgrim's Progress" was written. Mrs. Tabor spoke with pride about Harlington's link with the great evangelist and I was not surprised to learn that the Bunyan window in Harlington Parish Church was the gift from her and Major Tabor.

I'm sure Mrs. Tabor would have been interested if she had been alive fifty seven years later to learn about The Tinker's Trail taken by Harlington Parish Paths Partnership members (P3) on 11th June 2000. John Bunyan, a tinker by trade, mender of pots and pans, undertook his evangelistic walks cross country, walks which covered Harlington to Samsell near Westoning, amongst many others. The P3 group sought and followed the Harlington route, taking them past the old Production Tools factory of World War II with Bunyan's Oak long since dead in their vicinity with the replacement oak planted in 1988 by Dr. David Bellamy.

The recollection of tea-time with Mrs. Tabor also brings back memories of her family. She and Major Tabor had three children: John, Pamela and Elizabeth, the latter known as "Cooee" in the village. We are left to our own conclusions as to why! Cooee was a friendly soul and full of life, love and laughter.

She became a mannequin; she certainly was tall and very slim. After her marriage she lived in Ireland. Pamela, who was a Cordon Bleu in cooking, was often seen round about the village with her dog, a dachshund, this after the family pet, a dalmatian died. When Pamela married at Harlington Parish Church, she carried a most beautiful bouquet of heliotrope delphiniums. Children's and young impressionable people's memories often latch on to certain things and mine certainly latched on to these! The church choir members and bell ringers were guests at the reception at Harlington Manor. My father attended, accompanied by my mother.

The afternoon spent at the Manor left me with plenty of food for thought. I felt that not only should I tell the children in my writings about Mrs. Tabor's antiques, although I knew I could get interesting stories out of them, but it would be a great opportunity to give them a local history lesson on John Bunyan. It sounds a bit of a mixture, but it went down well, so much so that one of the little lads who was a member of my page came into the front office and asked to see Uncle Geofree because he wanted to know more about THAT OAK TREE. He wanted to climb it himself! What was I to do about that one, I wondered! A bit of quick thinking was needed here and I sailed down those impressive looking stairs with all the confidence in the world. I wasn't going to be caught out. I told the laddie that Uncle Geofree was out but that I was his secretary (Lord, forgive me, I prayed silently!) But that little one grinned happily at me and then came the BIG ONE. 'Corr,' he said. 'I bet you climbed the tree, too, didn't yer?' I had to admit that I had. Well, THAT wasn't a lie! He went away quite cheerfully, leaving me, however, with a drawing of Uncle Geofree as he thought he looked. The drawing was of an elderly man with whiskers and smoking a pipe! There were many chuckles in the reporting room when I showed the picture around. 'One day you may look like that,' someone said. I ignored the remark.

The antiques series, which lasted several weeks, was about a young boy, a nephew of Uncle Geofree's, who lived in a part of the Bedfordshire countryside which had links with John Bunyan. During the summer months, however, he stayed with his uncle in the nearby town. Uncle Geofree had a friend who owned an antiques shop and together they visited him and listened to the stories he told them about the antiques he had collected. Each week I took Mrs. Tabor an issue of "The Tuesday Pictorial" containing the next story in the series published in Uncle Geofree's page. The only way I can describe that lady's reaction to seeing her antiques in print and thus made famous is to say in today's language that she was "tickled pink" or "mighty chuffed!" She had never had a freeby before. She had always had to pay. And the reporters? They enjoyed the series too and I often caught them reading Uncle Geofree's Children's Page after that, with a few chuckles here and there. I suggested that they might like to become members. I was told not to be cheeky!

Chapter Twelve

Called To Serve

The Second World War was still raging when I reached the age of nineteen and I knew that my time had come to leave my days of journalism behind for a while. I felt frustrated by the thought at first, but when my call-up papers arrived I began to look forward to gaining experience of a different life somewhere other than my country existence in the village of Harlington. I had hoped to be sent abroad, much to my mother's horror, but my medical grade was one degree under the A1 required for overseas service. And then at my interview in Luton I expressed a desire to be drafted into Public Relations work in whatever service I found myself. That was fatal. No-one must ever ask, I was told, and I would be sent into whatever service I was most needed by at that time and do the work required of me. It happened to be the Auxiliary Territorial Service (A.T.S.) I ground my teeth at this as it was not my choice, but on discovering during my service years that Her Royal Highness, Princess Elizabeth, now our Queen, had chosen to join this service, although she had no need to be in any service at all, I felt considerably encouraged. I met a girl who had managed to get into the service she had hoped for, the W.A.A.F. (Women's Auxiliary Air Force), because, she said, the colour of the uniform would match her eyes! I couldn't say the same about my khaki!

I was not the only girl to be called up from Harlington and find herself wearing the khaki uniform of the A.T.S. My childhood friend Brenda from Pretoria Cottages also experienced life in that service, this after she had already taken a nursing career at the Alexandria Children's Hospital, Stockwood Park, Luton. She left nursing to join her sister, Gwen in the A.T.S. and after radar training she found herself on a gun site. At one point her career took her to Camberley where she met the then Princess Elizabeth who trained as a driver. After her A.T.S. career Brenda was in the Land Army and it was then that she met her husband and went to live in Cheshire. The years rolled away and I did not meet her again until a few years ago. She is now living in Blackpool.

Another Harlington friend of mine, this time from my early adult years, also saw service in the A.T.S. on an Ack-Ack site near Mumbles in Wales. Topper married Reg. Chappell when he returned from being a prisoner-of-war in Japanese hands with her father. Reg is featured in chapter nine of this book. Topper was a very gifted person in music and ballet, which was perhaps why, before her call-up she was employed by Farmer's, the Music Centre in Luton.

One day I found myself on my way to Guildford Training Centre for the life in khaki that lay ahead of me. In my bag was a small book, an edition of the Bible's New Testament presented to me by the then vicar of Harlington, Revd Thomas Crowther-Green. It was one of many copies presented by the churches throughout England to those who were joining the Services. From then on I always carried mine on my person wherever I went. It was usually tucked in my khaki uniform pocket. On arriving at the Training Centre I had to collect my Army issue of clothing from the stores, along with many other new recruits (at this stage we were called "Rookies," an American expression!). Like most young girls of my age I had

91

never worn a vest before, so that item of clothing went straight into the Army chest that served as a locker by my bed in the requisitioned house where I was to live. The pantees were not too bad; thankfully scanty, silky-rayon but in a sort of greenish khaki, so most of us wore our own from civvy street, although it was strictly against the rules and if we had been caught wearing them we would surely have been permanently on a charge! It was a good thing, then, that we didn't have "knicker inspection while worn!"

Brenda, nurse

Every day, up early, we had Physical Training wearing brown shorts and orange coloured tops, brown plimsolls and ankle socks. It was a bit cool first thing in the morning, but I'm sure it did us all good and got rid of some weight off the fat females - of which I was not one at that early stage of my life! - only to put it on perhaps after our energetic hour by being served doughnuts just oozing with jam along with hot mugs of cocoa. And we were usually so hungry by then that I don't remember anyone ever refusing them.

Brenda, A.T.S.

At the end of our training we had a Passing Out Parade on the vast parade ground at Guildford. It was a magnificent sight. Unfortunately, I had to wait for my own passing out because I had made friends with a girl who had Scarlet Fever. As my bed was next to hers, I had to go into Sick Bay with her, much to my frustration. When the day came for the parade I should have been on, I stood on a toilet seat to watch from the window - and promptly got stuck down the toilet when one foot slipped, the toilet seat not having been put down and I had not got time to rectify the matter. I was rescued by a nursing orderly.

At my own Passing Out Parade a short while after, I was proud to be marching behind the Queen's Own Regt. band, our Senior Commander directly after them riding side-saddle on a beautiful white horse. It was evident that she was an experienced horsewoman. We all had to look immaculate, with hair well above our collars, our brass buttons gleaming on our well pressed uniforms and our unglamorous hats completely straight and not cocked over one eye as I saw some of them worn in my future days. This was something I vowed never to do because it lowered the tone of our Service, a Service that was one to be proud of. For off duty hours we had been issued with forage caps in brown and orange, to wear if we wished to do so, but I preferred to wear the flat hats in khaki, although they were rather severe but in a design which seemed to suit me better.

At the end of our time at Training Centre we sat a Selection Test to see what we were really most suited for and to mark our intelligence! I was being tested for secretarial work, and when I passed muster I squirmed, wondering how boring it was to be after journalism. As it happened I found it very interesting and yet another experience to add to the list.

A temporary posting as a secretary to Southlands College, Wimbledon, a training centre for Army officers, was my first experience of life in the Service. This was while I was waiting for my permanent posting to come through. A girl dispatch rider became my friend. I thought she was extremely brave delivering messages to London, as the VI bombs, the "Buzz Bombs" as they were called, were falling all around. My friend and I often walked over Wimbledon Common on our off duty hours and that was when I had my first experience of a VI bomb. We heard it approaching - "chug chug, chug chug" - and jumped into a dried up ditch for some protection in case it exploded. But it passed overhead and with sighs of relief we scrambled out of our safe place - although I doubt it would have been of help to us if there had been an explosion! Then, to our horror, the flying bomb turned and headed straight back towards us and Southlands College not far away. This was one of the bombs just before the V2s were used (you couldn't hear those approaching at all because they were silent.) Our noisy VI - "chug chug. chug chug" - suddenly shut off and exploded on the College itself and many Army and A.T.S. personnel were killed. That experience was something I vowed never to tell my mother about. She would have been horrified, although of course she was always aware of the danger I was undergoing. My father had had experience of the First World War, having served at Passchendaele and coming home suffering with Shell Shock from which he did not recover for a number of years, so he was able to accept such news as an inevitable part of the war.

My permanent posting came through some time after. It was to Camp Commandant's office, War Office, Eaton Square. While there I worked amongst members of the Civil Service who were very kind and friendly. At that stage I was billeted in a flat in Paddington, but had to sleep with my platoon of K. Company, A.T.S. London District in the crypt of St. Peter's Church (Paddington). There were not enough bunks for all of us, so some of us were accommodated on the tombs for sleeping. It did not seem to bother anyone; after all it was not the dead we had to worry about but the living - those who were sending the Flying Bombs over London. The city was getting a full blasting! I was fortunate, though, that I had a bunk bed, albeit that it was extremely hard, and in St. Peter's crypt I would often think back to my comfortable bed at home in Harlington and long for the safety of that quiet little village.

Shortly afterwards we were moved to Chelsea in requisitioned houses that had been the homes of gentry. It was an area that suited me, particularly as I loved the artistic atmosphere of the surroundings and the Chelsea Pensioners in their red coats passing by. My room was at the top of our house conveniently next to a bathroom and when I looked through the window I could see into the room opposite where people were busy at their typewriters. I never ever discovered what that work was, but I was certain in my imagination that they were writers and I felt well and truly at home, absorbing the feeling.

It was right at the end of the war that I received a transfer to another part of the War Office, to Hobart House, not far from Victoria station and with it came promotion. The Princess Elizabeth's records were kept in this branch of the War Office. Her aunt, Princess Mary the then Princess Royal, was our Chief Commander.

It was very convenient to be near Victoria station, for I could catch a train to Teddington from there and spend weekends with relatives of my mother. But most weekends were spent at home in Harlington, perhaps taking the last train up the line from St. Pancras, this after the theatres reopened after the war. I loved to spend an evening at a theatre even on my own, when I was able to acquire a free ticket from the War Office theatre ticket clerk. I had already taken advantage of the Army Education Scheme and after winning a bursary to the Francis Martin College of Music and Dramatic Art, then at Tottenham Court Road, I was becoming more and more involved with theatre studies, gaining a number of medals and a diploma. But my mother was not pleased, pointing out that I had trained as a journalist and I should continue in that career. I feel now, so many years later, that she was right. Anything to do with theatre is very dicy and can bring a lot of disappointments and heartache. As it happened I was able on my return to civvy street to put my theatre knowledge gained in the A.T.S. to good use with my journalism.

When the end of the war was announced I was home on leave. I had about eighteen months more to do to the end of my service. There were many soldiers to be brought home for demobilisation and others, younger lads mostly, to be sent out for the clearing up process. Harlington village wasted no time in celebrating the announcement that the war had come to an end. They gathered on the Square to dance to music that was provided. My friend Topper was also home on leave and as the boys were not yet home there was a shortage of male partners and people hung back, perhaps too shy to take to the "floor" just outside the Manor in the central part of the village. So Topper and I gave demonstrations of ballroom dancing and included the Jitterbug, frowned on by some of the older members of the community. I thought my mother would be cross with me, but no, this time I was excused and she did not say 'I never know what she's going to do next!' Maybe she had resigned herself to it at last.

All this time that the war had been on, my very first friend of early childhood days, Joan, had been doing her bit for her country, making uniforms for the Army and Air Force at a firm called Eastex in Luton, a very responsible task indeed, for what would our boys have done without their Service clothes to wear? Everyone served their country in the village in their own respective way.

When an Armistice service was held in Harlington Parish Church after the war I was again home on leave, this time just for the weekend, so I was able to attend still in my khaki uniform. One other person in Service uniform was also present, a soldier, Aubrey Baker who was serving in the Army. His parents lived along Barton Road, opposite the lovely hills. It was a proud but humble moment for us when our names were read out during the roll call of those in the Services.

War Memorial, Harlington.

Arriving back in London for my last stretch of service life, I was called to see our Junior Commander, who informed me that an A.T.S. girl was required to broadcast a talk on "Make Do And Mend" at the B.B.C. and she wished to send me to audition. The subject was not my strong point. I always lost patience if I had to put a stitch in anything, although I knew what to do. I had never felt so nervous in my life as I sat in the BEEB studio with the microphone in front of me. But when I started to talk I surprised even myself that my voice never wavered. 'It's in the bag!' I thought gleefully as I returned to Base. But what a shock I got when my Junior Commander had to tell me that the girl who had been chosen came from Lancashire. Junior Commander was as disappointed as I was and the explanation she gave me was that the B.B.C. had required someone with a dialect to give the broadcast colour and it seemed I had not got one. How I wish I had given them a bit of old Bedfordshire countryside which can be very broad! It would seem my voice production training at the Francis Martin College had paid off a bit too well!

Approaching demobilisation, I had to make my way to Guildford once more to hand in my kit. Certain items could be kept if desired, or I could have a sum of money instead. I chose the money - I was weary of khaki and never wanted to see the colour again, so once back in civvy street, I spent a whole lot of my coffers instead on some really super clothes for my continuation of life with the Press, with the help of my auntie Mabel Asbury who supplied a quantity of her clothing coupons to add to the ones I had been issued with. One item in particular made a big hole in my expenditure - a beautiful evening dress cut on Grecian lines in a pretty shade of green, but I had to have it because I knew I would need it for some of the occasions I would be attending now I was going back as a senior reporter. I was allowed to keep my kit bag and it came in handy through the years ahead. It had a strong handle and was very roomy. But how I wished I hadn't got it with me on my demob journey back to Bedfordshire from London! It was quite a weight, mainly because I was travelling home with quite an assortment of things inside it, having been on a goodly shopping spree before leaving the city.

I stepped on to the train that was to take me away from my service life quite late at night. I THOUGHT it was the fast train to St. Albans, then slow all the way up the line to Harlington. The last train at night. I THOUGHT I would arrive home as I had so often done before and burst in at the door to find my faithful mum waiting there, my sister and dad tucked up in bed. What a shock for me when the train stopped at St. Albans, then starting up again, gathered speed to become a fast train ALL THE WAY UP THE LINE TO BEDFORD! It was dark outside of course, so on looking through the carriage window I couldn't see where we were and it was a terrific shock when the train pulled up and I heard "Bedford" being called out. I alighted. No-one about, just a very dim glow on the station.

Then I saw another light in the station and I called out 'Hallo.' A voice answered me and the ticket collector appeared, looking surprised. 'I didn't know there were any passengers,' he said, 'but I always have to call out just in case. This is the last train.'

The man looked very sorry for me but offered no solution to my plight; stuck in Bedford, no train back to Harlington, no taxis available at that time of night. What was I to do? Then I had a brainwave, if such it could be called. My friend Topper had a grandma living in Bunyan Road. I had been there often with her and knew where her house was - in daylight! Would I be able to find it in darkness and dead of night? Bunyan Road, on the way out of Bedford. Could I make it? I felt I could if I was able to leave my heavy kit bag in the station office. The ticket collector said yes, of course. He would be on early duty the next morning and I could collect it then. So I set off in the darkness, my heart beating very fast indeed, imagining all sorts of things happening to me, a young girl out on my own, if there were any nasty men about. All the time I had been in London I had never felt like that. I hurried as fast as I could in the direction of Bunyan Road, instinct guiding my steps. On arrival I hammered desperately on Grandma Birch's door. A face appeared at an upstairs window. Grandma Birch herself! I told her what had happened. In a second she was downstairs, had let me in and fixed me up to sleep on the settee, promising that her son, Topper's Uncle Reuben, would take me to the station the next morning and put me on the first train to Harlington. Strangely enough, I slept very well that night and the next morning Uncle Reuben took me to Bedford station and saw me off with my kit bag collected from the ticket office. Down the line at last to Harlington. With great relief I arrived home and flung myself in at the door, kit bag first. 'Child,' said my mother anxiously, 'wherever have you been?' When I told her the full story she shook her head and gave a big sigh, words failing her.

That night I went to bed early. But before settling down in my own nice cosy room I leaned out of the window and looked towards the distant hills as I had done in my childhood and many times since. A wonderful feeling came over me. I took a deep breath of good old Harlington air. "Aaaaah." It was indeed good to be HOME!

Chapter Thirteen

Back to Beds

Walking through the door of Home Counties Newspapers Ltd (the Old Luton News paper) after being away for three years seemed very strange to me. This time it was the side door in Alma Street, Luton, not as the first time, the front door in Manchester Street. The side door led to the very old, creaking stairs, so different from the ones in the front office that I had climbed on my first day as a little cub reporter a few years previously.

Along a landing I approached a new reporters' room, more spacious than the old one that had looked out on to the Alma Cinema. We now had a good view of the Co-operative stores across the road and the bus station (but I still used the train service from Harlington to Luton). I entered the room with some trepidation, wondering if there would be anyone there who would remember me. So many reporters were returning from their wartime service that some of them had to be moved to the firm's branch offices in Hitchin, Leighton Buzzard, Watford, Harpenden and so on. But I found a number of old faces there who gave me a warm welcome, plus two females who had not been there when I had left. We soon became buddies, glamorous Pat and pretty little Jean who was four years younger than myself. Jean was still at the cub reporting stage and doing the tasks that I had done before I left. She was a happy, carefree kid, hilariously funny in the things she said. It was not surprising then that the bloomer of bloomers rolled off her tongue while ringing round the vicars by phone, as I had once done.

'Hallo,' she trilled one morning down the mouthpiece. 'Is that the Revd. Wilkinson Widdle?' (His name was Wilkinson RIDDLE!) 'Oh, ha,ha,ha!' came back the jovial voice from the other end. Our chief reporter, Harry Middleton who had taken over from dear old Buckie who had long since retired and sadly had passed away, reprimanded her severely. 'Jean! Apologise!' 'Oh, dear, I'm so sorry, Revd. Wilkinson Widdle,' trilled Jean again, sounding not a bit perturbed. 'Oh, ha,ha,ha, ha!' (from the phone). Was the chief reporter cross! And was Jean's face red by the time he had finished with her. But the Revd. gentleman was a jolly vicar, full of humour. I remembered him well from the old days. Later, just before I left the firm to be married, Revd. Wilkinson Riddle became the vicar of St. Mary's, Sundon. He retired some time in the 1950s.

Jean was a great little friend. She loved to come home with me to Harlington on our days off, which we always tried to get together. We took long walks in the countryside which was wonderful for her as a "townie." One of them was through the old railway bridge of my childhood days and up towards Wick Herne, with its rabbits hopping about and playing. It hadn't changed much. Then we would take a different way home from the railway bridge, creeping under the wire that separated a path running along by the railway embankment from a large field to the bottom of Sundon Road. Now it is all the residential development of Park Leys. The path was very long and narrow and at the end of it we came out at the top of Sundon Road, just before the Square.

Sometimes Jean and I would take a walk through the old allotments where my Grampy Lane once had a vegetable plot. This led us to the part known as Goswell End, a part of Harlington with considerable history. When we walked there it was a fairly straight, long road with a large field to the left in which stood an old building that had once been Goswell End House, timber framed with stone window surrounds and dated from the late 16th to early 17th century. (Harlington In Camera, Russell Preston and Old Harlington In Camera (2) Russell Preston and Stephen Castle.) Some have incorrectly thought this to be the old Manor House before the one built in the centre of Harlington, known as Harlington House in which Major and Mrs. Tabor lived in my young days, but further on at the top of East End (Upper East End) ancient foundations are shown in a photograph in Old Harlington In Camera (2) which look suspiciously like the moated site of an original Manor House late 13th to early 14th century (and indeed it is recorded by Harlington Heritage Trust in their Brief History of Harlington, December 1999, Millennium Issue Newsletter No.75, that the original Manor House was built at Upper East End at that time.)

Goswell End Ruined Home

If we had taken our walk over the field to the left by Goswell End House ruins - which I'm sure Jean would have loved to do if only we had had time- we would have come to what remained of Forder's Brickworks. I had been there many times and remembered the derelict cottages there where a family of boys had once lived with their parents. Their name was Bastow and the lads went to Harlington school at the same time as I had done. Brickwork stopped on that site about 1906, but foundations of the cottages can still be seen.

Jean was always intrigued by the history of Harlington, the John Bunyan story, the old homesteads, the little school that I had attended as a very small child, so different from the large schools in Luton. Sometimes I became quite exasperated answering her questions. She was rather like a child asking "Why, when and where!" I did not know all the answers and I still don't today, but I have learned a lot since my walks with Jean. I just wish I had known the story of a row of little homes opposite Goswell End House. Jean would have said it was so romantic and I think it really was... Their history has been told to me by a person of the farming Giles family so prominent in the village throughout the years, who have been connected through their ancestry with these homesteads known as Adelaide Cottages. They were built sometime in the 1900s. Like Pretoria Cottages mentioned in chapter eight they were to house farm workers of the Giles' family, and were thus named by the farmer Giles of that time after his dear wife. Maiden name, Noake(s).

Further along Goswell End Road Jean and I came to the entrance to the old recreation ground where little Joan and I in years past used to use the two swings (it now sports more of Harlington's housing development!) and just beyond there were bee hives owned by Cllr White who lived with his wife and adult daughter Dorothy along the Barton Road. Then there was nothing but the long road until we came to an old cottage almost in ruins where the uncle of my little friend Joan of those earlier years had lived, Uncle Harry. Two Giles' farms were on the left, Horsehill and Upper East End farmsteads and here Jean and I turned to the right and made our way home to Sundon Road via Barton Road with its lovely view of the hills and cut across Bury Orchard.

Goswell End Road

One day Jean said she would love to walk to the hills. I had told her so many stories about our childhood picnics and it had whetted her appetite to see for herself at close range the site where the fir trees grew and where we had made our camp fire and cooked those sausages that had sizzled in the pan! So, with a small khaki pack from my Service days on my back containing sandwiches, apples, biscuits and some chocolate, we set off. Turning left at the spring where the watercress still grew, we walked along the narrow road that was little more than a lane, called "The Bottoms," a name which made Jean giggle until I reminded her that, well, it WAS the bottom of Harlington! We came to the old gate on the right that let us into the field and down to the spot where Piggot's farm had been before the Army firing range had destroyed it during the war. We stopped for a rest there before tackling the steep climb up to where the fir trees grew. It gave me time to look around and reminisce. Perhaps not a sensible thing to do, for it set the old nostalgia working. No ducks and no sound of geese cackling, warning us off and no Miss Dorothy Piggot to serve us milk and eggs - not that we needed them with our sandwiches. But with Jean babbling excitedly away beside me I was brought back into the present. At the top of the hill were numerous couples lovingly entwined around each other in the glorious early autumnal sunshine. The air smelled of pine, bracken and of the nuts that were just about ripe and ready for gathering. It was the wonderful perfumed air I will always connect with "Up the Firs!"

After a long rest Jean and I made our way across the stretch of hills towards the top of Moleskin Hill, Streatley, down to Sharpenhoe. It was certainly a few miles to Harlington and home, but we were not a bit tired. We passed the old Harlington Grange Mill on our way. Just past Sharpenhoe it still stands, although not now used, timber framed and dating from the 17th century. Part of the mill house has been demolished, but a modern bungalow by the side of it is lived in. Jean had brought her camera with her, a Brownie I think it was, very simple to use and so elementary compared to those in this day and age! She had been snapping things all the way we had come and the Old Mill was going to be her prize photograph. Next came Burgoyne's Market Garden, now Mill End Nurseries, and then we rounded the corner by the old Production Tools building, or remembered perhaps as Carboloy/Sandvik and we were well on our way home. Of course, I made sure to point out the old John Bunyan tree! She thought I was very honoured to have been born in the little village of Harlington (little then, but not now!) and she told everyone back at the "Luton News" what a wonderful place it was to live in. Jean was so romantic!

Grange Mill

This lovely, sparkling little friend of mine met with an untimely, tragic death just a year after her first wedding anniversary. My memories of her are very precious to me and I know there are Harlington villagers even today who remember her for her happy smile and vibrant personality. Not only those in Harlington, but in Luton also, especially Luton News reporters of the old firm who might still be around.

Country life seeped back into my veins very quickly, and memories of London dimmed somewhat, although I will always enthuse over the theatres and art galleries, strolls in St. James' Park and walks by the Thames embankment. Journalism took over with a vengeance with some very interesting jobs appearing on the agenda. Theatre studies at the Francis Martin College of Music and Dramatic Art in Tottenham Court Road, London, taken while I was in the Forces were turned to excellent measure when I became theatre and music critic for the "Luton News". Through my activities in that quarter I met Miss Bone of the music shop at that time for string instruments in Manchester Street. She formed the Luton Mandolin Band and as I was a mandolinist she asked me if I would become one of her players. I refused, however, because I thought it would interfere with my work on the newspaper, but she kept me in the background as a reserve.

I was given many political meetings to report and it was then that I found it was not so advantageous to be considered one of the fastest shorthand speed writers on the reporting staff! The other one was the chief reporter himself, so I usually ended up doing the wretched political jobs, especially when Mr A. T. Lennox-Boyd MP for Mid Beds came to Luton. He was said to be the fastest speaker in the House of Commons. The meetings went on until very late and I literally fell from the train when it reached Harlington station. Again that long dash up the road, across the Square and down Sundon Road to my home at midnight and in darkness! The next morning would find me arriving on Harlington station at the last minute, my train to Luton coming up the straight and into the station. My hair would be dishevelled and I would be panting for breath and everyone on the platform would be shouting 'Come on, Edna. Late again!' Well, of course I was. I was tired. The station master would look at me askance, but say nothing as he waited for me to board the train so he could blow his whistle for off! I knew my father would be told about it, though, when he came on duty.

And then one day my reporting days were over. I left to marry the then Circulation Manager who later became General Manager with Sales and Distribution. It was he who helped his boss, Mr. John Gibbs, joint managing director of Home Counties Newspapers Ltd, to pack the propaganda leaflets,

Nachrichten Fur Die Truppe, which were printed at Luton during the war and dropped by Americans over the German troops - the Leaflet Bombs they were called. The full story can be read in "Luton At War", the book compiled by the Luton News in 1946, first published in 1947, and recently reissued in two volumes. I am very proud that I knew a number of the staff at the Luton News who worked on this highly esteemed project. One person in particular is impressed upon my mind, Mr. A.F. Pope, who personally supervised the compilation of the book. Known to us reporters as "Old Popie", despite this nickname he was very highly respected. He was a brilliant journalist and sub-editor and there's no doubt that when we came under his fire because he considered our work was not of the standard he required of us, it was because we deserved it. But I have to say his "bark was worse than his bite" and did us good in our career as journalists. A pity there are not more Mr. Popes around in the newspaper world today!

Andrew Wilsher

There's no doubt about it that had I not left the Luton News in March, 1949, I would have had the task of reporting for my paper one of Harlington's most spectacular events, the opening of the Village Hall in 1950!

Chapter Fourteen

Village Spectacular

The village's history of many years passed before my eyes as I stood on the Square at Harlington on Saturday, 9th September 1950. I had just heard Mr. A.T. Lennox Boyd, M.P. for Mid Beds, give the address at the opening of the Village Hall to the vast gathering of parishioners and those who had once lived in the village and who had returned to witness the spectacular event. I was one of the latter. Having left Harlington on my marriage only a short while before, 1 was living in a neighbouring village, so I was able to return each week to spend some time with my parents and say hello to my close relatives and friends.

Village Hall

The opening of the Village Hall was an exciting time for me. I had observed the events that had been held to collect money for the building of it and indeed I had taken part in some of them in the years that had led up to the very special day that had at last arrived! It was unusual for me, though, to have to stand and watch another reporter from my newspaper, the old "Luton News" busily taking down the speeches of those gathered on the platform. That task would surely have been mine if I had not left to be married, but I couldn't help thinking how relaxing it was to see someone else doing the job while I took my ease, just absorbing the scene at my leisure!

The photographer was George Gurney, the chief photographer of the "Luton News" at that time, but now long since passed on. I had been out on many newspaper jobs with him. George was so well known in the town and country areas of Bedfordshire and photographs taken by him are still used today in the local press and magazines. I knew he would record for posterity the grand opening ceremony in superb photographic style. Not only for the future generation, but for those of us, myself an example, who were at that time young would be the senior citizens looking back at those pictures. Little did I think that I would survey another scene, the 50th birthday celebrations of the opening of that Village Hall in millennium year when another pageant would take place! But to Village Hall event number one...

There must be Harlingtonians other than myself who cut out and kept what was a wonderful report of the village spectacular when it appeared in the "Luton News" on 14th September 1950. They will be able to refresh their memory from it, but there will be many who will not be able to do so, especially the young ones of today, so a few facts will not go amiss, I hope, although the list of characters portrayed in the pageant is far from complete here.

On the ceremonial platform with Mr. Lennox Boyd were his wife, Lady Patricia and Mrs. Gertrude Tabor of Harlington House (Harlington Manor). Among other dignitaries were Mr. Harry Bonner, the then chairman of Ampthill Rural District; Major S. Whitbread, National Playing Fields Association; and representatives of the National Council of Social Service, the Service that gave a grant of £2,000 towards the Hall which cost £2,892 18s and 4d. to build. And a fact of extreme importance of course is that the Hall was built by the Harlington firm of Messrs. W.H. and L.F. Justice. Architect, Mr. C. Gurney Burgess.

Mr. Peter Whiskin introduced the speakers, of whom one was Lady Mander, who delivered a message in the absence of her husband, Sir Frederick Mander.
Mr. Whiskin and his wife, Cllr. Esme Whiskin- my helpful friend of journalistic days - had worked so hard with others to achieve the goal, the Village Hall, that it must have afforded them great satisfaction to know that it had at last been reached.

The history of Harlington down the ages was presented in grand pageantry and included past Royalty of England; John Bunyan who had brought everlasting fame to the village; Nigel d'Albini (granted the Manor by William the Conqueror); church dignitaries and monks; and a deservedly special mention must be given to the child plaiters of yesteryear and those who represented industries and service men and women of World Wars One and Two.

Among the people taking part were those who, fifty years on took part also in the "second time around" highlight, including members of my own family. My third cousin Alan was a "monk". The thought of him in this respect has made me chuckle, for he was a saucy (in the best of senses), lovable lad with a round, rosy face and sparkling eyes who took a delight in teasing me. He was a very young monk, but now he would surely make a wonderful "Friar Tuck" with his rotund figure and kindness of heart so many years on! Alan's mother, Joyce Hart, my mother's cousin, and his grandmother Mrs. Ada Harris - sister to my Grandma Lucy rode in the magnificently turned out coach owned by Mr. George Mossman of Luton, the coach pulled by his team of four beautiful horses. Mr. Mossman died some years ago, but his collection of coaches and carriages are now on public exhibition at Stockwood Park, Luton. Alan's grandfather, Mr. William Harris (my great -uncle Will through marriage) was also in the procession as the Parson.

Mossman's Coach

Henrietta Maria Wentworth, who became the wife of Charles 1st, was portrayed by Joan Giles, who was exquisitely attired in a costume identical to that worn by the original Henrietta and shown in pictures in Luton Public Library. Joan had researched diligently to achieve the clever effect.

Ecclesiastical Procession

Sideshows were in abundance in Bury Orchard and in the evening there was a wonderful firework display, followed by a dance.

It has been thought that Kit Rogers of Harlington was the first bride to hold her wedding reception in the new Village Hall when she married Dennis Read, a police officer. This was not so. It was unfortunate that their wedding and reception had to be booked well in advance for it turned out to be the very day that Harlington eventually decided to hold the Village Hall opening. They therefore had to rebook the reception elsewhere and they chose The Bell Inn, Westoning. Kit was a very close friend of mine. I was extremely upset when she died in 1985 in Cornwall where she and Dennis lived on his retirement from the Police Force. He retired as Detective Superintendent at Police Headquarters, Kempston. Bedfordshire. Dennis lived on until at

Joan Giles

the age of eighty he died in February 2000, also in Cornwall. Their daughter Suzanne lives in Germany.

The opening of Harlington's Village Hall, 1950, was certainly a very spectacular event to be remembered down the years.

Chapter Fifteen

Millennium

Through the following years I kept my tryst with Harlington, visiting my parents who lived there until they died. My husband Andy and I had bought a three hundred years old cottage in Maulden (Bedfordshire), so we were on the doorstep for Harlington until one day the link was broken for a while when we took off for Scotland on my husband's retirement. He wanted to fish for salmon ALL the time not just twice a year on holiday; he had many friends up there through his Army days at Auchtermuchty, Fife and his love for Scotland was deep and strong. So it was that one day I found myself gazing out of my bungalow window in Perthshire on to the beautiful Grampian foothills. But they were not the hills of home; they were not the Chilterns, the Sharpenhoe Clappers and the hills known then as Markham, now Sundon Hills. I was homesick for them and the little villages in Bedfordshire, particularly the village of Harlington.

When eventually I was whisked back to my home county (remembering how picturesque it was then, unlike today with all the industrial estates and houses that have sprung up) I was overjoyed. It was not to Harlington though, but to Silsoe, "just around the corner" with its own colourful history connecting it with the Earls de Grey who came over with William the Conqueror and Wrest Park with its beautiful mansion and gardens. Harlington has a link with Silsoe through the first steeplechase in 1830 which started from St. Mary's Church, Harlington and ended at Wrest Park. The winner was ridden by Captain Macdowall. The horse's name? "Wonder."

We were approaching the new millennium fast, but I had arrived back on homeground in good time for it, starting off with my visit to Harlington to view "The Pilgrim's Progress" display in the autumn of 1996 which featured in the first episode of this book. It was followed on quickly by my attendance at an unusual and deeply stirring play with singers and music on that same theme, delivered and presented by a group called Speakeasy and Good Fortune and adapted by Beric Norman at the Church of St. Mary the Virgin.

Something of great importance and honour for Harlington was to be read in Harlington Village Magazine "Contact", May 1997. English Heritage released a new map of England that showed Harlington to be as one of just two sites commended by English Heritage in Bedfordshire. It shows St. Mary's Church (late 13th to 14th century) and states that John Bunyan was arrested for preaching nearby and that a window in the Church is dedicated to him. It was one of the several national commemorations to mark the 1400th anniversary of the landing of St. Augustine on our country's shores.

Achievements have come fast for Harlington in recent years. In October 1997 Mrs. Mary Rutherford the Parish Clerk was awarded Bedfordshire Community Charity's "Clerk of The Year" award at Great Barford Village Hall and at the same event Harlington's "Contact" Magazine was awarded a certificate of merit. The village had another "double" with, first, the award as Bedfordshire's Village Of The Year in the National Village Of The Year Award, 1998, sponsored by Calor Gas and The Daily Telegraph. Harlington then represented Bedfordshire in the Regional Competition in London. Then, in September 1998 in Thurrock, Essex, Harlington received a silver rose bowl and certificate for being The Most Improved Entrant Of All Classes in East Anglia In Bloom Competition.

Gradually I learned more and more about the happenings in my old village, organisations and societies that had sprung up since I had left. Harlington had expanded in more ways than one! There was still a Ladies' Bright Hour not altered overmuch but certainly without a stove to set their place alight! The Methodist and St. Mary's Church Sunday Schools and Services had certainly become more inspired through the years; the Literary Society that had started up sounded pretty good to me and I knew that if I had been living in Harlington I would most certainly have joined; the Arts and Crafts Society annual exhibition both my husband Andy and I now like to attend. Drama is very strong in the village, with a great deal of talent showing itself; and Harlington Festival Society has been favoured with two visits from Gerald Dickens, a direct descendant of the great Charles, and I have enjoyed the two performances given by him; and Harlington now has its own Heritage Trust, founded in 1981. And so the list goes on and when the new millennium showed itself round the corner everyone got busy preparing their own contributions for it, so that the year was very colourful and highly enjoyable - not forgetting, of course, what it was really all about, the birth of Jesus Christ.

At St. Mary's Church the Vicar and his team had so much to do in the spiritual run- up. For the church workers there were very important tasks ahead and perhaps the biggest of all was preparing and repairing the Church bells. It was often very worrying, but at last everything was set for midnight December 31st, when Harlington's five very ancient bells were joined by a very new treble bell to sound over the village. The Hone Bell, the new treble bell, had been generously bought with money given by a church member, Mr. Arnold Hone, and was cast at the Bell Foundry, Whitechapel in 1997, but midnight,

December 31st ,1999 was the first time the bell was sounded and a special peal was composed for the occasion by the Vicar, Revd. Steve Williams. Sadly, Mr. Hone was not present at that wonderful moment. He died on 14th July 1999, aged 88.

A unique offer by St. Mary's (Harlington) PCC at a reasonable price were the miniature replicas of the mediaeval bell, the Bell, cast in c.1440. There were only a few on offer, so those who were fortunate enough to acquire one will have a collector's item indeed!

Like most churches, St. Mary's was open throughout the evening with the chancel lit by candlelight for prayer and meditation, with hot drinks served at the West End of the Church and a T.V. turned on to show what was happening elsewhere in the world. At midnight Harlington's 17th century clock was heard for the first time in a quarter of a century and then it was time for a superb fireworks display in Bury Orchard.

Millennium gifts of candles were distributed to each house in the village by Harlington Christian Council to be lit at midnight on December 31.

And so to the Village Hall 50th Birthday Pageant held on 9th September 2000 in Bury Orchard...

As I stood watching, a very colourful procession wended its way round Harlington on what turned out to be an extremely hot day; I was pleasantly surprised to hear the Church clock chime. I did know about the clock chimes' and bells' special programming, making it different from any other village I knew to mark the time of day. Tunes were of hymns and other suitable music.

The opening ceremony was performed by Brian Golby, the then Mid. Beds District Cllr., dressed as Lord of Harlington Manor, 1670, in a very eye catching costume complete with a feather, waving flamboyantly in his hat!

Brian Golby

As in fifty years past, the pageant was historical and the Main event of the day, although it was different from then, was still very spectacular and colourful. In particular I was greatly impressed by the Stilt Walkers in their bright yellow costumes. To walk around the Village in that manner was certainly something and they stood out dramatically. The tug-of-war between the two village pubs the "Old Sun" and the "Carpenters Arms" brought forth some mirth and the Milton Keynes Pipe Band added to the celebratory spirit. Many spectators were fascinated by a Stunt Kite (bird) display. Arts and Crafts drew the many spectators into the Parish rooms where refreshments were served and in the evening a Barn Dance was held in the Village

Hall. And at these 50th anniversary celebrations who should I meet again but my friend of childhood days, Joan, who had lived next door to me all those years ago!

Stilt Walkers

A coach with a team of horses in the pageant is worthy of special mention. It was magnificently turned out as in the first pageant of fifty years previous. Among the passengers was Mrs. Eleanor Lee, widow of Cyril Lee, Wood Farm. Mrs Lee was a founder member of Harlington Women's Institute in earlier days and also their first president; and who should be sitting on the top deck but that little "monk" of yesteryear, my cousin Alan. But not as a monk. This time, now very full adult, he was himself! But Alan can portray characters with aplomb and through the years in addition to his main employment and especially after his retirement bringing him into the millennium he has obliged many people as a "Vac" Chimney Sweep which keeps him very busy- proof indeed that some people are still having REAL fires! He is in much demand, too, at weddings attending as Sweep in an elegant Sweep's "Dress Suit" with top hat for the occasion to bring the bridal pair good fortune. I believe this custom is an old one, although I don't remember my friend, the late Kit Rogers and bridegroom Dennis Read having a Sweep to bless their nuptuals fifty years past.

Votes for Women

Reminiscing on the years of my life now the new millennium is here, I find certain sadness encompassing me from time to time through the loss of dear friends who have died; Topper of A.T.S. days and the boy she married, Reg, who had been a Japanese prisoner-of-war. Those two took such an active part in the British Legion when they arrived back in Civvie Street, Reg being a standard bearer and both taking part in the Albert Hall ceremonies in London. The British Legion was so very dear to their hearts; Jean, my little journalist friend; and then there was Kit Rogers who had once lived in the Franklin's Coals house in Westoning Road, near the little cottage where I was born, after the days of Mr. and Mrs. Alfred Denton.

I have a great affinity with Harlington Church. My father's ashes lie in the shadow of the Church in the Garden of Remembrance, a short distance from where Shirley Williams, M.P. once planted an oak tree when visiting Harlington. The last I heard of Shirley's Oak, however, was that it was dying, although attempts were to be made to save it. (Shirley Williams' mother was Vera Brittain, who wrote the book "In the steps of John Bunyan" in 1950.)

But on a much brighter side of things, my friend Brenda is living in Blackpool and passes my way once a year when we recall together many memories of the village and our younger days.

I feel a big accolade is due to Kitty Chambers who played the organ at the Methodist Church when I was a child and these many years on is still playing it there at this time of writing. She is now in her eighties. Kitty once lived in one of the two cottages called "Mount Pleasant" at the back of the then Post Office, now "Pound Cottage." Her brother, Harry was a local Methodist preacher and her sister (Floss) married William Justice, one of the Justice Brothers who built the Village Hall.

With earliest thoughts of Methodist days come memories of Chapel Fetes when I often presented a bouquet to the lady who opened the event, giving her a deep curtsy and saying shyly, 'Please will you accept these flowers?' (I don't know what I would have done with them if she had said, 'No!') There was also a lovely lady who made icecream for the occasion. The strawberry was particularly delicious! This lady was known affectionately as "Auntie Church" and her husband, Mr. Joe Church, worked in Harlington railway station office.

Another link with the past was the planting of the yew tree by the daughter of the well remembered Methodist character,"Aunt Patti!" This was to mark the new millennium.

(Yew trees were offered to churches by the Conservation Foundation to commemorate the millennium celebrations.) Mrs. Flossie Willson (nee Stone), had the honour of planting Harlington's yew tree in St. Mary's churchyard towards the end of 1999. She, herself was 99 years old and Flossie was presented with a Harlington Millennium plate as a thank you gift for performing this ceremony.

Chapter Sixteen

The Spencer Painting: A Legacy

My father first told the family about the painting left to Harlington Parish Church of St. Mary the Virgin by its artist, past incumbent of the Church, Revd. William Spencer, D.D. 1894 - 1905. Beneath the painting the artist has written the words: Harlington in 1896. W. Spencer D.D. did it. The painting is therefore just over one hundred years old.

Throughout the story in this book I have sat for a few short minutes in the quiet of the mornings to collect my thoughts before writing and I have found my gaze drawn to the copy of this unusual picture on the wall of my lounge. I had never dreamed that it would ever be there. Whether the day has been dull or murky or if the sun has been brilliantly shining, I have never failed to be inspired by that painting, because it depicts the beginning of my own journey through life to the new millennium. The inspiration drawn from it has culminated in the story you have just read in this book.

The picture shows the little Victorian village school (now the Parish Hall) I attended first of all; Straw Plaiters House where my Great-uncle Charlie lived with his family; and not least the Church itself where my parents were married and my sister and I were baptised. It towers sentinel towards the sky, its entrance facing the beautiful distant Sharpenhoe Clappers and the once called Markham, now Sundon, Hills. But the main feature of this picture is its foreground. Between

Great-uncle Charlie's house on one side and the school building on the other are some very special people in small clusters, dressed in the attire of a hundred years ago. They are the village postman, the village baker, the milkman with a very old-fashioned milk cart to bring on nostalgia for those still living who remember how the milk was once brought round to their houses before milk bottles were used. The old milk churns show up very prominently in the little old horse drawn milk cart. Records state that George Gregory was the dairyman. But the character I like best is the coalman carting coal in a barrow. Now that really is something! According to Kelly's Directory, there were three coal merchants who served the area at that time. Remembering that Franklin's Coals had an office at the bottom of Station Road, Harlington, when I was a girl, it would seem most likely that Mr. Franklin, or rather an employee, was the deliverer of the coal in that barrow, even though it was unlikely that a coal office was in Station Road then. Two people are standing having a chat and there is even a little lad trundling a huge hoop almost as big as himself, giving him, I'm sure, as much pleasure as those computer games for today's children and much healthier, too, no doubt, with all that exercise! The headmistress of that day is seen looking over the school wall. As Mr. Apthorpe was the schoolmaster even then, she may be his wife, Mrs. Apthorpe, who also taught and I understand too that the vicar's own wife is amongst the little group of ladies and children in the corner by the school.

The most remarkable part of all, which makes this picture so outstanding, is that the incumbent, Revd. William Spencer, has portrayed himself walking by the archway at the entrance that leads up to the Church porch. An impressive touch! That Revd. gentleman was given the name "Moses" by his parishioners. Appropriately enough this, for he had a long white beard which can clearly be seen in the picture. I feel I want to walk round him and make my way up the path and into the Church and capture past moments in time.

Built of Totternhoe stone known as "clunch," the Grade 1 Church dates from cl300-l350, although an earlier church, perhaps wooden, is said to have existed before this. The first tower was 15th century but has now been replaced. Its clock is believed to date from 1750, maybe earlier, but it does not strike as it once did. In fact, for a long time it did not strike at all. But as you have read, it is programmed to play a tune mainly of spiritual merit when it tells the villagers the time now. There is also another time teller in its own special way, the sundial seen before entering the Church.

The picture on the wall of my lounge brings back a fond memory of my old Grampy Lane hurrying up the Church path and into the Church, wearing his stiff black bowler hat and dressed in his Sunday best suit, clutching a book. It would have been his hymn book, no doubt, for in those days worshippers were asked to bring their own hymn books if possible, as Church books were in short supply. The organ, rebuilt in 1958, has as its organist, as I am writing this, Mrs. Pearl Everett, a relative of mine. She has held that position a goodly number of years.

The present-day choir of St. Mary's retired in June 1998. (I haven't heard of one being formed since.) A church without a choir I feel is not quite complete and the thought makes me sad. In my father's day Harlington Church had a strong choir. My thoughts drift back to a certain night when I took off with our family dog from home to meet my father who was attending choir practice. A brilliant moon shone, casting an ethereal glow overall, merging with the light shining from the Church windows as I waited just inside the little gate leading into Bury Orchard. I stood listening to the choir voices rising and falling as they sang their anthem.

Another, to my mind, unfortunate happening was that a former vicar of Harlington removed the choir stalls and the pulpit, so that the people were in the nave of the Church. It is said that it was so that they would be nearer an altar, the side chapel altar being used. During the Revd. Stephen Williams' incumbency, however, a new altar was made from the fallen branch of the John Bunyan oak tree after the great storm in 1987 (see poem at the beginning of this book.) It is good, also, that some of the Church furniture is back in its rightful place, although not so the pulpit in the year 2000.

A parish church, of course, acts as a unique repository of gifts, dedications and memorabilia of many of the notable people and events in a village such as Harlington. Amongst the names of the past vicars listed in the Church is Revd. William Price Ind (Bill Ind) who was a very good friend of my father. Both had a great interest in sport and he and father often visited Lords Cricket Ground to watch the matches there. My father missed him a good deal when he died and he would not have been the only one, for Mr. Ind did much to promote sporting and other village activities. He was vicar of St. Mary's from 1945-1956. His grave is in Harlington's Barton Road cemetery. Mr. Ind's wife was a direct descendant of Elizabeth Fry, renowned for her prison reform work in her time.

There are many who will remember Mr. John Van Weenan, not only in Harlington, this because of his appearance, albeit reluctantly, on T.V.'s programme "Hearts of Gold," after leading a convoy of lorries taking aid to Albania. They may also have read his story in the book, "Task Force Albania: An Odyssey." Mr. Van Weenan, a resident at Harlington Manor (Harlington House) after the days of Major and Mrs. Tabor, gave a brass candelabra to St. Mary's Church. In February of 2001, Mr. Van Weenan was seen on T. V. by many viewers as the celebrity on "This Is Your Life."

Behind a wooden screen is the choir vestry. The screen has three panels, the first dedicated by Mrs. Tabor to her husband, Major Sydney Tabor, MC. (1876-1946); The middle panel, designed by Professor Richardson of Ampthill in memory of: Gertrude Mary Tabor (1874-1976); and the third panel, added later, to John Bentley Sydney Tabor, son of Major and Mrs. Tabor (1908-1967). When she left Harlington Manor Mrs. Tabor went to live with her daughter, Pamela at Kimpton, where she died just before her one hundred and second birthday. Pamela is also now dead. She will be remembered in Harlington by the name of Mrs. Daniels. After her husband died, she remarried and became Mrs. Hilton. Her second husband was a top game warden in Kenya. The yesteryears come flooding back as I write this - Mrs. Tabor and her connection with "Uncle Geofree" and Pamela walking her dachshund (dog) through the village, a story told in chapter eleven of my journalistic years. The other daughter, Elizabeth, known as "Cooee", has also died.

A very special feature of Harlington Parish Church is a Crucifix in the War Memorial Niche. It is described as an Oberammergau Cross. (Church records, 1969 Inventory). A memorial to the men who died in the first World War can be seen in the north aisle where, also, is the Lady chapel with its Flanders carved altar, one of the gifts of Mrs. Gertrude Tabor. Another of her gifts, the window dedicated to John Bunyan in 1929, is always of primary interest to visitors to St. Mary's, Harlington.

Amongst other memorial windows is one of great significance to the Church itself. It is to the memory of the incumbent of many years ago, Revd. William Spencer who lays at rest in the new cemetery, Barton Road. Not only was his time in Harlington fruitful for the village as a talented artist and dedicated vicar, but he was also the initiator in his day of Harlington's Village Magazine. A special edition was published in January 1996 in which the full story was told of how the present-day magazine came to be. This edition had an outer cover with its latter day title, "Contact. January 1896-1996. Harlington Village Magazine." There was then an inner cover, a reproduction from the time of Revd. William Spencer, with the words, "Harlington (Beds) Vol.1. Church and Parish Magazine 1896." Its title: "The Dawn Of Day." A Selective Blessing in the Church of England service for many years is to be found in The Common Book of Prayer, 1928. Beginning "Go forth into the world in peace" it ends, "Rejoicing in the power of the Holy Spirit Until the dawn of God's Eternal Day." The Spencer magazine those many years ago would seem to have been inspired by these words.

The present-day magazine "Contact" is still published monthly by Harlington Christian Council. One could say the title is more in line with today's world and reaches out not only to the people in the village but to those who were once resident there and have now moved away such as Jack Hewitt and his wife Margaret of the Kent family who once lived at Wood Farm. The couple now live in Barnstaple, north Devon, but Jack retains his memories of Harlington where he played tennis at the Old Vicarage in Church Road and helped mow the tennis court, lawn and banks round the court which overlooked the vicarage drawing room. He also remembers a building in which a carriage was kept but never used. What happened to it, he wonders? Perhaps someone somewhere knows.

Through "Contact" I read about the wonderful Art Conservation Award won by the Church of St. Mary the Virgin for the Spencer painting. The award was made by Woodmansterne Publications Ltd, publishers of Fine Art Cards in 1997. It was one of six paintings selected in their scheme to conserve pre-20th century paintings and it was listed as: "Church Road, Harlington in 1896 painted by the then incumbent,

Revd. W. Spencer, (whose nickname amongst his parishioners was Moses.)" Paul Woodmansterne, managing director of the family owned firm of Woodmansterne, was on the panel with four other judges: Lord Antrim, a former head of conservation, Tate Gallery; Donald Forbes of the National Galleries of Scotland; Diane Dollery, the Museum at Caerleon; and Janet Tamblin, Plymouth Museum & Art Gallery. The painting received a grant and renovation and after being returned to Harlington Church a special ceremony with celebratory lunch was held in The Garden Room, Westoning Road, Harlington. It was indeed an outstanding occasion, for amongst those present were relatives of the late artist and incumbent of St. Mary's, Revd. William Spencer. A limited number of copies on canvas were later sold for £50, each, £10 of which went to the Church. I was quick to buy one of the limited number of paintings, for I knew they would soon be sold. It epitomises for me the spirit of Harlington as it used to be in the years gone by. I hope that old Harlingtonions and those who have come to live in the village more recently will alike feel the specialness that this heritage has passed down the generations and that my personal memories have sought to recapture.

Books Published by THE BOOK CASTLE

COUNTRYSIDE CYCLING IN BEDFORDSHIRE, BUCKINGHAMSHIRE AND
HERTFORDSHIRE: Mick Payne. Twenty rides on and off-road for all the family.
PUB WALKS FROM COUNTRY STATIONS: Bedfordshire and Hertfordshire: Clive Higgs.
Fourteen circular country rambles, each starting and finishing at a railway station and
incorporating a pub stop at a mid way point.
PUB WALKS FROM COUNTRY STATIONS: Buckinghamshire and Oxfordshire: Clive Higgs.
Circular rambles incorporating pub-stops.
LOCAL WALKS: South Bedfordshire and North Chilterns: Vaughan Basham.
Twenty-seven thematic circular walks.
LOCAL WALKS: North and Mid Bedfordshire: Vaughan Basham. Twenty-five thematic
circular walks.
FAMILY WALKS: Chilterns South: Nick Moon. Thirty 3 to 5 mile circular walks.
FAMILY WALKS: Chilterns North: Nick Moon. Thirty shorter circular walks.
CHILTERN WALKS: Hertfordshire, Bedfordshire and North Bucks: Nick Moon.
CHILTERN WALKS: Buckinghamshire: Nick Moon.
CHILTERN WALKS: Oxfordshire and West Buckinghamshire: Nick Moon.
A trilogy of circular walks, in association with the Chiltern Society. Each volume contains
30 circular walks.
OXFORDSHIRE WALKS: Oxford, the Cotswolds and the Cherwell Valley: Nick Moon.
OXFORDSHIRE WALKS: Oxford, the Downs and the Thames Valley: Nick Moon.
Two volumes that complement Chiltern Walks: Oxfordshire, and complete coverage of the county,
in association with the Oxford Fieldpaths Society. Thirty circular walks in each.
THE D'ARCY DALTON WAY: Nick Moon. Long-distance footpath across the Oxfordshire
Cotswolds and Thames Valley, with various circular walk suggestions.
THE CHILTERN WAY: Nick Moon. A guide to the new 133 mile circular Long-Distance Path
through Bedfordshire, Buckinghamshire, Hertfordshire and Oxfordshire, as planned by the Chiltern
Society.
CHANGES IN OUR LANDSCAPE: Aspects of Bedfordshire, Buckinghamshire and the Chilterns
1947-1992: Eric Meadows. Over 350 photographs from the author's collection
spanning nearly 50 years.
JOURNEYS INTO BEDFORDSHIRE: Anthony Mackay. Foreword by The Marquess of
Tavistock, Woburn Abbey. A lavish book of over 150 evocative ink drawings.
COCKNEY KID & COUNTRYMEN: Ted Enever. The Second World War remembered by the
children of Woburn Sands and Aspley Guise. A six year old boy is evacuated from London's East
End to start life in a Buckinghamshire village.
CHANGING FACES, CHANGING PLACES: Post war Bletchley and Woburn Sands
1945-1970 Ted Enever. Evocative memoirs of post-war life on the Beds/Bucks borders, up to the
coming of Milton Keynes new town.
BUCKINGHAM AT WAR: Pip Brimson. Stories of courage, humour and pathos as Buckingham
people adapt to war.
WINGS OVER WING: The Story of a World War II Bomber Training Unit: Mike Warth.
The activities of RAF Wing in Buckinghamshire.
JOURNEYS INTO BUCKINGHAMSHIRE: Anthony Mackay. Superb line drawings plus
background text: large format landscape gift book.

BUCKINGHAMSHIRE MURDERS: Len Woodley. Nearly two centuries of nasty crimes.

WINGRAVE: A Rothschild Village in the Vale: Margaret and Ken Morley. Thoroughly researched and copiously illustrated survey of the last 200 years in this lovely village between Aylesbury and Leighton Buzzard.

HISTORIC FIGURES IN THE BUCKINGHAMSHIRE LANDSCAPE: John Houghton. Major personalities and events that have shaped the county's past, including Bletchley Park.

TWICE UPON A TIME: John Houghton. North Bucks short stories loosely based on fact.

SANCTITY AND SCANDAL IN BEDS AND BUCKS: John Houghton. A miscellany of unholy people and events.

MANORS and MAYHEM, PAUPERS and PARSONS: Tales from Four Shires: Beds., Bucks., Herts. and Northants: John Houghton. Little known historical snippets and stories.

THE LAST PATROL: Policemen killed on duty while serving the Thames Valley: Len Woodley.

FOLK: Characters and Events in the History of Bedfordshire and Northamptonshire: Vivienne Evans. Anthology of people of yesteryear -arranged alphabetically by village or town.

JOHN BUNYAN: His Life and Times: Vivienne Evans. Highly praised and readable account.

THE RAILWAY AGE IN BEDFORDSHIRE: Fred Cockman. Classic, illustrated account of early railway history.

A LASTING IMPRESSION: Michael Dundrow. A boyhood evacuee recalls his years in the Chiltern village of Totternhoe near Dunstable.

ELEPHANTS I'LL NEVER FORGET: A Keeper's Life at Whipsnade and London Zoo: John Weatherhead. Experiences, dramatic and sad, from a lifetime with these well-loved giants.

WHIPSNADE MY AFRICA: Lucy Pendar. The inside story of sixty years of this world-renowned institution. Full of history, anecdotes, stories of animals and people.

GLEANINGS REVISITED: Nostalgic Thoughts of a Bedfordshire Farmer's Boy: E.W. O'Dell. His own sketches and early photographs adorn this lively account of rural Bedfordshire in days gone by.

BEDFORDSHIRE'S YESTERYEARS: The Rural Scene: Brenda Fraser-Newstead. Vivid first-hand accounts of country life two or three generations ago.

BEDFORDSHIRE'S YESTERYEARS: Craftsmen and Tradespeople: Brenda Fraser-Newstead. Fascinating recollections over several generations practising many vanishing crafts and trades.

BEDFORDSHIRE'S YESTERYEARS: War Times and Civil Matters: Brenda Fraser-Newstead. Two World Wars, plus transport, law and order, etc.

DUNNO'S ORIGINALS: A facsimile of the rare pre-Victorian history of Dunstable and surrounding villages. New preface and glossary by John Buckledee, Editor of The Dunstable Gazette.

DUNSTABLE DOWN THE AGES: Joan Schneider and Vivienne Evans. Succinct overview of the town's prehistory and history - suitable for all ages.

HISTORIC INNS OF DUNSTABLE: Vivienne Evans. Illustrated booklet, especially featuring ten pubs in the town centre.

EXPLORING HISTORY ALL AROUND: Vivienne Evans. Planned as seven circular car tours, plus background to places of interest en-route in Bedfordshire and parts of Bucks and Herts.

PROUD HERITAGE: A Brief History of Dunstable, 1000-2000AD: Vivienne Evans. Century by century account of the town's rich tradition and key events, many of national significance.

DUNSTABLE WITH THE PRIORY: 1100-1550: Vivienne Evans. Dramatic growth of Henry I's important new town around a major crossroads.

DUNSTABLE IN TRANSITION: 1550-1700: Vivienne Evans. Wealth of original material as the town evolves without the Priory.

DUNSTABLE DECADE: THE EIGHTIES: A Collection of Photographs: Pat Lovering. A souvenir book of nearly 300 pictures of people and events in the 1980's

STREETS AHEAD: An Illustrated Guide to the Origins of Dunstable's Street Names: Richard Walden. Fascinating text and captions to hundreds of photographs, past and present, throughout the town.

DUNSTABLE IN DETAIL: Nigel Benson. A hundred of the town's buildings and features, plus town trail map.

DUNSTAPLE: A Tale of The Watling Highway: A.W. Mooring. Dramatic novelisation of Dunstable's legend of Dunne the Robber - reprinted after a century out of print.

25 YEARS OF DUNSTABLE: Bruce Turvey. Reissue of this photographic treasure-trove of the town up to the Queen's Silver Jubilee, 1952-77.

DUNSTABLE SCHOOL: 1888-1971. F.M. Bancroft. Short history of one of the town's most influential institutions.

BOURNE and BRED: A Dunstable Boyhood Between the Wars: Colin Bourne. An elegantly written, well illustrated book capturing the spirit of the town over fifty years ago.

OLD HOUGHTON: Pat Lovering. Pictorial record capturing the changing appearances of Houghton Regis over the past 100 years.

ROYAL HOUGHTON: Pat Lovering. Illustrated history of Houghton Regis from the earliest of times to the present.

WERE YOU BEING SERVED?: Remembering 50 Luton Shops of Yesteryear: Bob Norman. Well-illustrated review of the much loved, specialist outlets of a generation or two ago.

GIRLS IN BLUE: Christine Turner. The activities of the famous Luton Girls Choir properly documented over its 41 year period from 1936 to 1977.

THE STOPSLEY BOOK: James Dyer. Definitive, detailed account of this historic area of Luton. 150 rare photographs.

THE STOPSLEY PICTURE BOOK: James Dyer. New material and photographs make an ideal companion to The Stopsley Book.

PUBS and PINTS: The Story of Luton's Public Houses and Breweries: Stuart Smith. The background to beer in the town, plus hundreds of photographs, old and new.

LUTON AT WAR - VOLUME ONE: As compiled by the Luton News in 1947, a well illustrated thematic account.

LUTON AT WAR - VOLUME TWO: Second part of the book compiled by The Luton News.

THE CHANGING FACE OF LUTON: An Illustrated History: Stephen Bunker, Robin Holgate and Marian Nichols. Luton's development from earliest times to the present busy industrial town. Illustrated in colour and mono.

WHERE THEY BURNT THE TOWN HALL DOWN: Luton, The First World War and the Peace Day Riots, July 1919: Dave Craddock. Detailed analysis of a notorious incident.

THE MEN WHO WORE STRAW HELMETS: Policing Luton, 1840-1974: Tom Madigan. Fine chronicled history, many rare photographs; author~served in Luton Police for fifty years.

BETWEEN THE HILLS: The Story of Lilley, a Chiltern Village: Roy Pinnock. A priceless piece of our heritage - the rural beauty remains but the customs and way of life described here have largely disappeared.

KENILWORTH SUNSET: A Luton Town Supporter's Journal: Tim Kingston. Frank and funny account of football's ups and downs.

A HATTER GOES MAD!: Kristina Howells. Luton Town footballers, officials and supporters talk to a female fan.

LEGACIES: Tales and Legends of Luton and the North Chilterns: Vic Lea. Mysteries and stories based on fact, including Luton Town Football Club. Many photographs.

THREADS OF TIME: Shela Porter. The life of a remarkable mother and businesswoman, spanning the entire century and based in Hitchin and (mainly) Bedford.

FARM OF MY CHILDHOOD, 1925-1947: Mary Roberts. An almost vanished lifestyle on a remote farm near Flitwick.

STICKS AND STONES: The Life and Times of a Journeyman Printer in Hertford, Dunstable, Cheltenham and Wolverton: Harry Edwards.

CRIME IN HERTFORDSHIRE Volume 1 Law and Disorder: Simon Walker. Authoritative, detailed survey of the changing legal process over many centuries.

JOURNEYS INTO HERTFORDSHIRE: Anthony Mackay. A foreword by The Marquis of Salisbury, Hatfield House. Introducing nearly 200 superbly detailed line drawings.

LEAFING THROUGH LITERATURE: Writers' Lives in Herts and Beds: David Carroll. Illustrated short biographies of many famous authors and their connections with these counties.

A PILGRIMAGE IN HERTFORDSHIRE: H.M. Alderman. Classic, between-the-wars tour round the county, embellished with line drawings.

THE VALE OF THE NIGHTINGALE: Molly Andrews. Several generations of a family, lived against a Harpenden backdrop.

SUGAR MICE AND STICKLEBACKS: Childhood Memories of a Hertfordshire Lad: HarryEdwards.Vivid evocation of gentle pre-war in an archetypal village, Hertingfordbury.

SWANS IN MY KITCHEN: Lis Dorer. Story of a Swan Sanctuary near Hemel Hempstead.

MYSTERIOUS RUINS: The Story of Sopwell, St.Albans: Donald Pelletier. Still one of the town's most atmospheric sites. Sopwell's history is full of fluctuations and interest, mainly as a nunnery associated with St.Albans Abbey.

THE HILL OF THE MARTYR: An Architectural History of St.Albans Abbey: Eileen Roberts. Scholarly and readable chronological narrative history of Hertfordshire and Bedfordshire's famous cathedral. Fully illustrated with photographs and plans.

THE TALL HITCHIN INSPECTOR'S CASEBOOK: A Victorian Crime Novel Based on Fact: Edgar Newman. Worthies of the time encounter more archetypal villains.

THE BOOK CASTLE
12 Church Street, Dunstable
Bedfordshire LU5 4RU
Tel: (01582) 605670 Fax (01582) 662431
Email: bc@book-castle.co.uk
Website: www.book-castle.co.uk

The
Book
Castle